SEWING
Face Masks, Scrub Caps, Arm Slings, and More

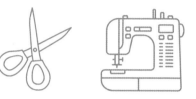

SEWING
Face Masks, Scrub Caps, Arm Slings, and More

Practical Projects for Comfort and Care

Angie Herbertson

Landauer Publishing

Sewing Face Masks, Scrub Caps, Arm Slings, and More

Landauer Publishing, *www.landauerpub.com*, is an imprint of Fox Chapel Publishing Company, Inc.

Disclaimer: Interfacing products are not designed for long-term use around the nose/mouth and their manufacturers have not tested the products for potentially toxic effects from long-term use. Include interfacing in your mask(s) if desired at your own risk, or feel free to omit when creating any mask project.

Project Team
Editor: Colleen Dorsey
Tech Editor: Amelia Johanson
Copy Editor: Amy Deputato
Designer: Llara Pazdan
Photographer: Mike Mihalo
Indexer: Jay Kreider
Illustrator: Sue Friend

ISBN 978-1-947163-66-9

Library of Congress Control Number: 2020914686

We are always looking for talented authors. To submit an idea, please send a brief inquiry to acquisitions@foxchapelpublishing.com.

Note to Professional Copy Services:
The publisher grants you permission to make up to six copies of any patterns in this book for any customer who purchased this book and states the copies are for personal use.

Printed in the United States of America
24 23 22 21   2 4 6 8 10 9 7 5 3 1

This book has been published with the intent to provide accurate and authoritative information in regard to the subject matter within. While every precaution has been taken in the preparation of this book, the author and publisher expressly disclaim any responsibility for any errors, omissions, or adverse effects arising from the use or application of the information contained herein.

INTRODUCTION

Sewing Face Masks, Scrub Caps, Arm Slings, and More presents simple projects and sew-ables that can easily be made and donated or given to loved ones. Each project is a teaching tool to walk the new sewing enthusiast through basic skills. The projects range from a simple, happy pillowcase to brighten up a hospital room, to a more advanced wheelchair caddy or scrub hat in bright fabrics. Learn stitching skills, how to work with a variety of tools and notions, and how to do patchwork, pleating, binding, reverse appliqué, and more. If you've always wanted to learn to sew, *Sewing Face Masks, Scrub Caps, Arm Slings, and More* lets you conquer the basics while making helpful projects for a better world.

CONTENTS

26

Cheery Adult Bib

30

Half–Hour Ear–Saver Headband

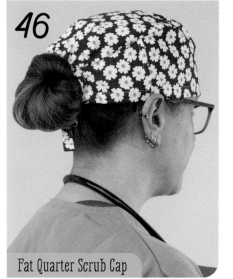

46

Fat Quarter Scrub Cap

50

Cooper Unisex Scrub Cap

54

Pleated Face Mask with Pocket

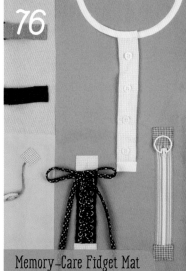

76

Memory–Care Fidget Mat

88

Arm Sling Cast Cover

34 Ponytail Scrub Cap

38 Tab Blankie

42 Stretch Knit Face Covering/Scarf

60 Shaped Face Mask

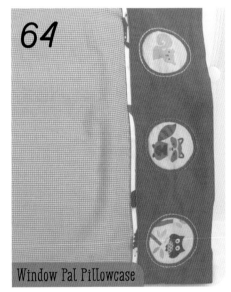

64 Window Pal Pillowcase

70 Quilt-As-You-Go Lap Blanket

94 Fat Quarter Wheelchair/Walker Caddy

These projects are great for...

Everyone

The Elderly

Healthcare Workers

Children

PART 1

Sewing Basics

Before you jump into all the great projects in this book, take some time to familiarize yourself with the materials, tools, and techniques you'll need to make the projects—it's all covered here. If you have limited experience sewing, read this section carefully and then start with an easier project, such as the Cheery Adult Bib or the Pleated Face Mask with Pocket. If you're an experienced sewer, you can still learn something from this section and get a head start on collecting all the materials you'll need—plus you may pick up some tricks or get introduced to helpful products that you never knew you could use!

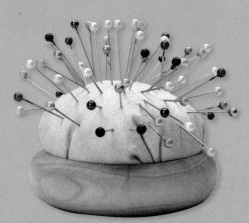

Materials and Tools

There are thousands of different sewing supplies and notions, and it would take an encyclopedia-sized book to cover them all. Here, I'll address the supplies needed to make the projects in this book. Some, like a seam ripper, are optional. Who knows—you might be the first sewing enthusiast ever to not have to rip out a single seam. (Spoiler alert: that person doesn't exist.) Other supplies are required to successfully sew from start to finish, and I've included a few non-traditional items as well. I've listed some of my favorites, but there are many different brands available. The one absolute must is a good-quality sewing machine, preferably with button and buttonhole functions, a zipper foot, an edge foot, and the ability to move needle positions. I recommend researching all the top brands and reading consumer feedback. It's absolutely essential to invest in a quality machine if you want to truly experience the joy of sewing.

High-Quality Fabrics

If you're going to take the time to pour your creativity into a sewing project, it's worth investing a little more in quality **quilting cottons, no-pill fleeces,** and **soft flannels**. You can often buy fabric in the form of **fat quarters** and **charm packs**, which can be good ways to purchase fabric for some of the projects in this book. Many of the projects in this book can be made with a yard or less of fabric or a fat quarter, which is a piece of fabric cut crosswise from ½ yard (45.7cm) of fabric and which generally measures 18" x 22" (45.7 x 55.9cm). Because quilting yardage width can vary, occasionally that 22" (55.9cm) width is slightly wider or narrower. A charm pack is a bundle of 5" (12.7cm) pre-cut squares; a set of these is used for the Quilt-As-You-Go Lap Blanket.

Needles

There are different needles for machine sewing and hand sewing with their own names and sizing systems. There are dozens of machine sewing needles crafted for the types of fabrics with which you are working and even for the threads you're using: ballpoints and stretch needles for knits; sharps and quilting needles that are helpful for layers and batting; denim (jeans) needles; leather needles; embroidery needles for machine embroidery; and topstitching needles designed to pierce fabrics easily. Each needle type's eye and point are designed for specific threads and purposes to enable threads to pass through the needle and the needle to pass through the sewing surface successfully.

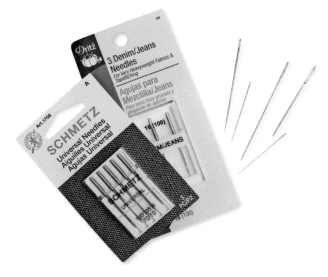

For machine sewing, an **80/12 universal needle** is used to sew nearly every project in this book, as all the projects call for medium-weight woven fabrics. The one exception is for the Stretch Knit Face Covering/Scarf, for which a **ballpoint needle** is used. A ballpoint needle can be used with fleece as well. Use a **topstitching needle** whenever your project calls for topstitching, and a **sharps or quilting needle** for stitching through several layers or batting. A good rule of thumb is to choose finer/narrower needles (75/11 or below) for lightweight fabrics and larger/wider sizes (90/14 or above) for heavier-weight fabrics.

The only three hand sewing needles required to complete the projects in this books are a **size 10 sharps** needle for stitching down quilting binding, a **size 9 embroidery/crewel needle** for stitching on snaps and buttons (it has a slightly larger eye) and for embroidery stitching on the Window Pal Pillowcase, and a **large-eye darner needle** to accommodate cord elastic for the Memory-Care Fidget Mat. There are dozens more hand sewing needles out there, from beading to darning to upholstery needles, and they're named for the point, eye, length, and diameter. The wrong type of needle can result in poor stitch quality if you are doing tapestry, cross-stitch, needlepoint, or fine embroidery work, for example. For sewing on snaps, buttons, or bindings, as you'll be doing for projects in this book, generally a medium-length sharps or crewel will suffice.

Thread and Floss

All-purpose, 50-weight, good-quality polyester sewing thread in colors to coordinate with your fabrics will work for all of the projects in this book. I personally like the brands Coats & Clark™, Gütterman, and Mettler®, as they are of a strong quality, rarely have a burr (a rough spot that might catch in the needle eye), and are less likely to break or shred, but you can experiment with any brand you like to see what works for you.

As with needles, threads come in a multitude of types. You can choose **machine quilting or topstitching threads** when executing those particular steps in a project if you prefer, or you can stick with the same all-purpose thread described previously. Some sewing enthusiasts prefer to use cotton thread only, although

it does tend to break over time more readily than a polyester alternative. **Hand embroidery thread** is often called "embroidery floss" and is usually comprised of up to six strands. You can separate them to use as many strands as you want at a time. For purposes of this book, embroidery floss is used as an option to decorate the Window Pal Pillowcase and to tether the doily to the pocket of the Memory-Care Fidget Mat so it doesn't get lost.

Seam Rippers

Seam rippers range from tiny-handled traditional options to ergonomically designed tools. Prices vary depending on the design, but you should always have at least one on hand to remove stitches much more easily than if you were using scissors, as well as for opening buttonholes. They do dull over time, so replace them after significant use.

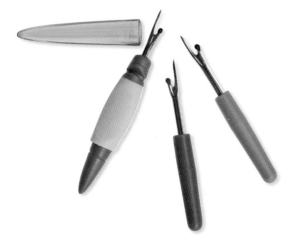

Seam Gauges and Seam Guides

If you sew regularly, you know how helpful a 6" (15.2cm) metal **seam gauge** can be. With a sliding pointer that holds its place at the precise measurement you want, it's invaluable for marking placement of buttons and buttonholes, checking strap placement, and doing quick checks on your seam allowances, binding widths, and smaller fabric pieces. Seam allowance is the amount of space between the edge of the fabric and the stitch line. Binding width is how wide the binding will finish on the front side around the edge of your quilt or other bound project. Because you often fold the binding

to the back side of your project and either pin, secure with quilting clips (not used in this book), or baste with fabric glue, you can use a seam gauge to check that the width is consistent before sewing the binding down by hand or machine.

Seam guides are ⅓₂" (0.08cm)–thick adhesive strips that adhere to the throat plate (machine base under the presser foot) on your machine. They leave no residue and can be removed and re-adhered several times before losing their effect. Using a seam gauge, you can measure an exact stitch width and position your seam guide on the throat plate, then run the edge of your fabric along the seam guide as you stitch to achieve the exact seam allowance you want. My personal favorite seam guide is produced by Guidelines™ 4 Quilting.

Sewing Scissors, Pinking Shears, and Rotary Cutters

Every sewing enthusiast needs a top-quality set of **sewing scissors/shears** that is used only for cutting fabric. There are a many brands and styles, traditional and ergonomic, so the choice is yours. Just make sure your pair is sharp and marked for fabric use only. **Pinking shears** are optional, but they are good for reducing seam bulk,

Buttons

Shirt buttons are standard buttons with holes through the center; **shank buttons** have a shank or protrusion sticking out of them, with the hole through the shank. While shank buttons must be sewn on by hand, shirt buttons can be attached by sewing machine, by either selecting the buttonhole option or selecting a zigzag stitch and reducing your stitch length to 0. Always remember to drop your feed dogs when sewing buttons on by machine. Both shirt and shank buttons are used in this book: the Memory-Care Fidget Mat uses four-hole ¼" (0.6cm) shirt buttons as well as ⅝" (1.6cm) plastic shank buttons.

which is why you'll often find charm packs for quilting pinked along the edges. If you sew more than a little, and especially if you quilt, a **rotary cutter** is essential. Team a rotary cutter with a quality clear ruler, and you will be able to make perfectly sized cuts all day long. Keep sharp, replaceable blades on hand and dispose of dull blades safely as soon as you find you're not cutting completely through your yardage.

Elastic

If you're making face masks, you can use strips of fabric binding for ties, but most users prefer the ease of **elastic loops** to stretch around the ears. Elastic can be flat (strips) or round (cord). Tiny elastic, smaller than ⅛" (0.3cm) wide or in diameter, tends not to hold a mask in place very securely. If it's all you have, you can double it or braid it. Just make sure to tie a small knot on each end so it doesn't pull out of your stitch line. Flat ¼" (0.6cm) elastic is easier to insert and stitch over by machine; however, I find that ⁵⁄₃₂" (0.4cm) cord is the most comfortable to wear. You will also need elastic for the bead block on the Memory-Care Fidget Mat and for the Half-Hour Ear-Saver Headband.

Bias Tape and Binding

Bias tape is a narrow width of fabric cut on a 45-degree angle to the selvage (lengthwise edge) of the fabric. The diagonal cut is "on the bias," which lends stretch. Bias enables the strips to curve without tucking or puckering. For bias tape, several strips are often joined together to create length. The join, too, is done at an angle to preserve the bias effect. It's commonly used to bind seams or finish edges.

Binding is essentially the process of enclosing the edges of a quilt or other project. You can buy products called "quilt binding," and the term is sometimes used interchangeably to refer to bias tape. However, not all quilt binding is cut on the bias. In fact, most quilters do not cut their binding strips on the bias, as they are not working around curved edges.

Bias tape can be purchased in single or double fold. Single-fold bias tape has the long raw edges folded to the wrong side for finished edges. If it is labeled ½" (1.3cm), that is the finished width with the edges folded under. It's often stitched around a neck edge or armhole (curved edge), folded to the back side, and secured with a hand or machine stitch so you do not see it on the outside of the project. Double-fold bias tape is folded in half a second time, not quite in the center, so that one side is slightly wider. This way, you catch the wider side on the underneath (back side) of your project when stitching on. Double fold is positioned or folded around the raw edge of a project so half of the tape is visible on the front and half is on the other side, then stitched to secure it close to the folded-under edges.

Projects in this book use both single-fold ½" (1.3cm) and double-fold ½" (1.3cm) bias tape. Several projects call for **binding**, which can be cut on the straight of grain from coordinating fabric, not on the bias (45-degree angle). To make your own single-fold binding, cut strips five times the width of your finished binding. For example, if you are finishing with ¼" (0.6cm) binding, cut binding strips 1¼" (3.2cm) wide. Determine the length by measuring around your project and adding 10" (25.4cm) for corners and joining the ends. For double-fold binding, cut the width of the strips ten times the finished binding width—for the previous example, 2½" (6.4cm) wide. A ½" (1.3cm) **bias tape maker** comes in handy to make ¼" (0.6cm) ties for masks.

Interfacing and Stabilizers

The face masks, fidget mat, and wheelchair caddy all call for an optional stabilizing element, called **interfacing**, to be added permanently to the fabric. There many different brands of interfacing, sold in packets and by the yard. It's always helpful to have at least 1 yard (0.91m) each of heavyweight, medium-weight, and lightweight interfacing in your sewing room. The iron-on interfacing used for the face masks also adds a layer of defense. A lightweight fusible interfacing (such as Pellon® P44F) is used in the pleated masks. A heavier-weight iron-on interfacing (Pellon 71F Peltex® or Pellon ES114 Easy-Shaper®) is used in the shaped masks to help them retain their form. Heavier-weight interfacing is also used on the back of the fleece blocks for the fidget mat and nearly all the pieces of the wheelchair caddy. The key to success when adhering fusible interfacing to fabric is to not iron, but to press in place, and to cut the interfacing pieces slightly smaller than the fabric pieces so that you're just catching the edges in your stitch lines.

Stabilizers serve a similar function to interfacing but are removed after stitching. Most often, they are torn away or washed away. Always use a tear-away stabilizer between the fabric and the throat plate when stitching machine buttonholes.

Batting

Batting is a lofted sheet of material that offers cushioning, dimension, and insulation between the top layer and bottom layer of a project, generally quilts or bags. **Cotton batting** is a little pricier than polyester batting, but working with a quality natural fiber leads to comfier results. Batting is sold in packages and by the yard; just make sure you purchase a piece that is at least 4" (10.2cm) larger than your project all around, as batting shifts during the quilting process.

Marking Tools

A **water-soluble** or **wash-away marker/marking pen** or air-soluble marker (if you're working relatively quickly) is in important tool for marking cut lines, stitch lines, button and buttonhole placement, and more. Always test your chosen marking tool on a scrap of your fabric before using it to make sure the marks will disappear.

Fabric Glues and Spray Adhesives

Easily top-ten sewing notions for me are **fabric glue** and **fabric glue pens**. Pins can pull your edges out of line, especially when sewing through several layers, but glue sets your fabric in place for straight, smooth stitching. In desperation, I've used a classic Elmer's glue stick to secure my hems, adhere trim, or tightly fold bias binding over raw edges in preparation for topstitching. However, non-fabric glues can gum up your needle, so keep a fabric glue stick on hand. Another "cheater" product, which I use on my Stretch Knit Face Covering/Scarf, is EZ-Steam™ II fusible tape. Rather than hand stitching the small opening used to turn the scarf right side out, I press back the edges of the opening, tuck a strip of this permanent fusible tape between the layers, and press. It is pressure sensitive and sticky on both sides, so you can reposition if needed before setting with heat.

Pins

Fine, **glass head pins** are the only way to go in general sewing. If you touch them with an iron, the colorful heads won't melt onto your fabric! You can also purchase **pins with larger heads**, which are popular in quilting and are easier to pick up and find when you inevitably drop them under your work area.

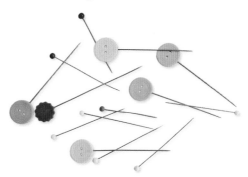

Temporary **spray adhesives**, such as Sulky® KK 2000™, temporarily bonds fabrics to appliqués, batting, stabilizers, and patterns. They disappear within a few days. I find it helpful to spray my batting surface when I'm using a quilt-as-you-go technique, such as in the Quilt-As-You-Go Lap Blanket project, smoothing one section down securely before attaching the next section.

Clear Rulers

If you've ever made a single quilt, you'll come to fall in love with **clear quilting rulers**. Like most sewing and quilting notions, they come in all varieties from different companies. A square ruler is ideal for cutting precise blocks. A longer, narrow ruler provides a firm, straight edge for rotary cutting and squaring edges. Here are the rulers and measuring tools I had on hand while making the projects in this book: a Fiskars® 3" x 12" (7.6 x 30.5cm) ruler, an OLFA® 6" x 12" (15.2 x 30.5cm) rectangle, a Creative Grids® non-slip 10½" (26.7cm) square, and a Creative Grids® non-slip Stripology ruler (made for use with a rotary cutter).

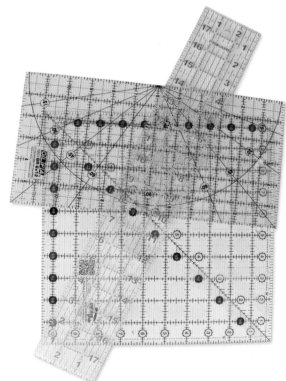

Tube Turners

Fasturn® **tube turners** come in a variety of sizes and are extremely helpful in turning fabric tubes right side out. They can be purchased in a set of six different tube sizes that range from ³⁄₁₆" (0.5cm) in diameter to 1⅛" (2.9cm) in diameter. If you want to make your own spaghetti bias for the Memory-Care Fidget Mat, the size #2 or #3 tubes are invaluable, and the #5 tube is helpful in making the Half-Hour Ear-Saver Headband.

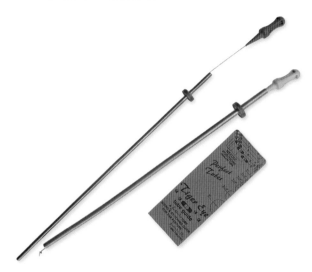

Miscellaneous Notions

The projects in this book utilize a wide variety of other **miscellaneous notions** that can be easily found in sewing stores or online. Here's the list, with the brands I used; you can of course use any particular products you choose.

- Parachute buckle for 1" (2.5cm) strap (Dritz®)
- Velcro® Sticky Back for fabrics (permanent), 1" x ¾" (2.5 x 2cm) ovals
- Large hook and D-ring for 1" (2.5cm) strap (Dritz)
- Adjustable slide buckles for 1" (2.5cm) strap
- 1" (2.5cm) webbing (Dritz)
- Zipper pull (Coats & Clark)
- All-purpose zipper, at least 14" (35.6cm) (Coats & Clark)
- Elastic flat braid, ¼" (0.6cm) (Prym)

Tip

Both high-quality and bargain tools can be good tools. Sometimes you'll get lucky and find a cheap tool that just seems to work perfectly for your needs. But if you're not pleased with a lower-quality item, try spending a little more on a higher-quality one for better results.

Techniques and Tips

Sewing enthusiasts create in endless ways. You may find a more effective approach for certain tasks than the person who taught you, or you might prefer their tried-and-true techniques. Technological advances in notions, tools, and sewing machines often change and improve the way we work, or a simple toothpick might do the trick in lieu of a fancier alternative. In this section, I've included some of the essential tasks you'll be repeating when making the projects in this book. Use it as a reference point as needed, or feel free to use your own preferred techniques to achieve what you want.

Edge Stitching

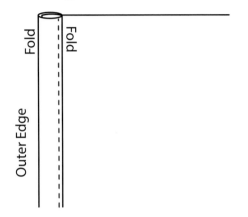

FIG. 1

Edge stitching is a decorative and functional reinforcing line of topstitching generally made just inside the edge of a fabric fold (fig. 1). It can be made in the same color thread, which is less noticeable, especially if you're still practicing your machine stitching, or in a contrasting thread for design interest. The stitch is done a scant (slightly less than) ⅛" (0.3cm) next to the fold, an exact ⅛" (0.3cm) next to the fold, or even just a few threads' width next to the fold. When using edge stitching to apply a binding where you want to catch the back of the binding in your bobbin thread line, I recommend using fabric glue to position and secure the binding an even width on both sides first, and I recommend stitching at least ⅛" (0.3cm) from the fold. Always take a few stitches and then check to make sure you are catching the binding on the back side. If not, adjust your needle position (if that is a function on your machine). Some machines come with edge-stitching feet, which can help in this task but are less helpful around turns.

Nesting Seams

FIG. 1A

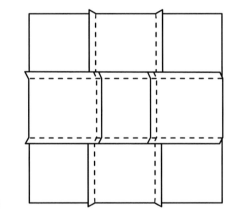

FIG. 1B

Nesting seams helps to eliminate any lumps or bulk in the seams, particularly on a quilt. It's common to quilting and essentially means to press the seam allowance *between* a set of joined blocks in one direction and the seam allowance on the set of blocks you'll be joining *to* it in the other direction (figs. 1a and 1b). It's a simple, time-honored technique for quilting, and it also helps layer your seam allowances in opposite directions to cut down on bulk in the front seam of a shaped face mask. So, for example, stitch the center seam of the Shaped Face Mask to the right, and stitch the same seam on the lining to the left. Place right sides together, aligning the seam lines, and place a pin just outside the seam allowance on each side of the seam to keep the pieces aligned when stitching.

Attaching Buttons by Machine

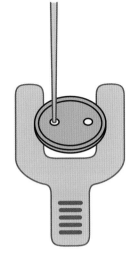

FIG. 1

FIG. 2

When sewing on buttons by machine, be sure to use the button spacer, which generally comes with the machine. This plastic spacer lies between the button and the fabric while the machine stitches the button into place (fig. 1).

If you don't have a button spacer, place a toothpick or a large safety pin underneath the button, out of the way of the needle path (fig. 2). You need to use a spacer of some sort when applying buttons to leave some room between the fabric and the button to insert through a buttonhole or, in the case of the Half-Hour Ear-Saver Headband, to the accommodate the elastic.

Generally, the holes in buttons are ⅛" (0.3cm) apart, so that is the width to set your zigzag or button application stitch. However, always test by manually turning the handwheel to check that the zigzag width will accommodate the button.

To keep smaller buttons from shifting, it can help to dab some fabric glue on the back side of your button before placing it in the sewing position. Always drop your feed dogs when stitching on a button by machine, or they will rise up and move your button.

Once the button is stitched, clip the threads on top of the button long enough to thread the ends through a hand sewing needle and thread to the back side of your project. Your machine should have a fix stitch—a function that essentially creates a secure knot by stitching up and down several times in the same hole—but if you want a safer application, knot the thread ends on the back side and clip them off.

Attaching Buttons by Hand

Everyone, regardless of their level of interest in sewing or their skill level, should know how to sew on a button. It's a simple life hack. Button thread is the best choice, but all-purpose sewing thread will work as well. Use a sharps needle with an eye that's comfortable for you to thread.

1. Cut the thread to approximately 24" (61cm), thread through the needle (doubled), and tie a knot at the ends (fig. 1).

2. Mark the placement of your button with a wash-away marker or stitch and insert the needle just to the left of the mark for a two-hole button or slightly up and to the left of the mark for a four-hole button (fig. 2). This keeps the knot hidden under the applied button, not on the back surface of your project.

3. Bring the needle back up right next to your starting point, insert the needle through a hole in the back of the button, and then slide the button down against the surface into place (fig. 3).

4. Pass the needle down through the opposite hole, through the fabric, to complete one stitch, and then slip a toothpick or a thicker darning needle underneath the stitch and against the button to use as a spacer. This keeps your button from being stitched too tightly against your surface. Continue stitching in one hole and out the other, pulling each stitch tightly against the spacer. Make six to seven passes this way (fig. 4).

5. Once you've made your last pass, remove the spacer and bring the needle up underneath the button between the button and the surface. Wrap your thread around the base threads at least five times (fig. 5a). Then insert your needle through your wrapping and back out, make a thread loop, and pass the needle through, pulling it tightly against the threads (fig. 5b). Clip off the end.

6. To apply a shank button, you do not need a spacer, because the shank serves as the spacer. As before, insert your knotted thread from the right side of your surface so the knots are concealed, wrap your stitching once the button is applied, and tie off the end in the same manner as described for two- or four-hole buttons.

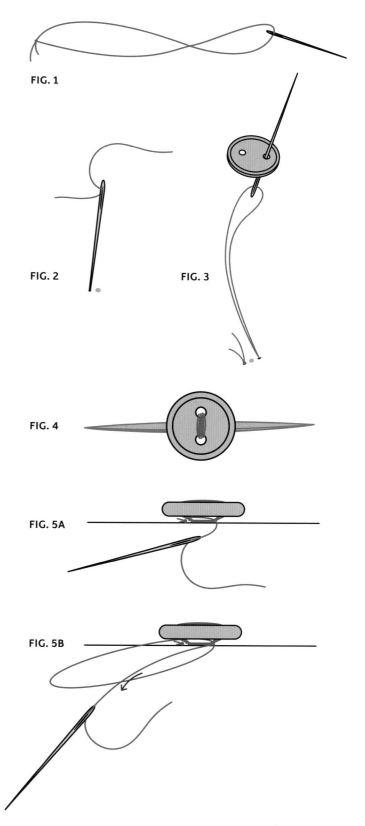

FIG. 1

FIG. 2

FIG. 3

FIG. 4

FIG. 5A

FIG. 5B

Chain Stitching

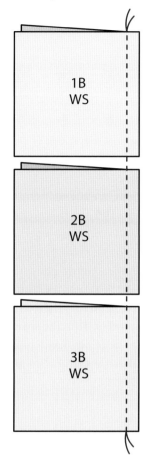

FIG. 1

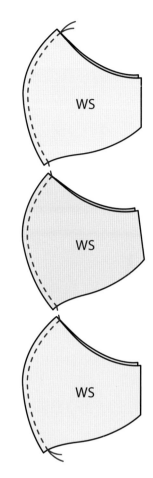

FIG. 2

Chain stitching is a common time-saving quilting technique whereby pieces to be joined are stacked right sides together and then stitched one after another without cutting the thread between them.

1. Place quilt squares in a pleasing order and label them on the back with a wash-away marker by column and row; for example, A1 through A7, B1 through B6, etc.

2. Start by joining the squares in column 1 to column 2, placing the A2 square on top of the A1 square, and stitching ¼" (0.6cm) down the right-hand side. Do not clip the threads at the end of your stitch line. Instead, stitch off the edge a few stitches, then feed the next pair (B2 on top of B1) through. Continue this technique until all the pairs in columns 1 and 2 are "chained" together (fig. 1).

3. In order to nest the seam, press the top pair's seam allowance to the right, and the next pair's to the left, alternating down the chain. Clip and then, depending on the next step in the construction process, stack and chain again, always remembering to place the section that will finish on the right side of the design on top.

While this concept is generally used in quilting, it also comes in handy when making face masks, Half-Hour Ear-Saver Headbands, or other simple items in multiples. For the Shaped Face Mask, for example, prepare and stack your mask pairs and lining pairs rights sides together and chain the center seams one after the other, making sure to fix your stitching when you start and stop on each mask (fig. 2). Prepare the joined pieces for the next step, stack masks and linings right sides together, and chain the seams across the top. Leave the masks joined and then chain the bottom seams before clipping the chain apart. All that remains is adding the elastic and ties to each mask, and before you know it, you've completed dozens.

Joining Binding Ends

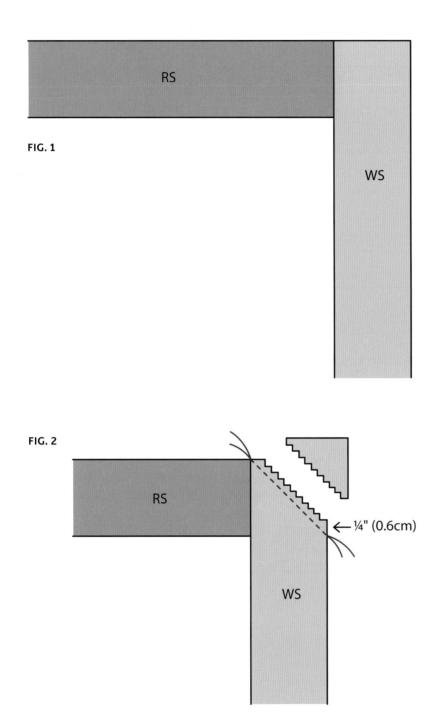

FIG. 1

FIG. 2

← ¼" (0.6cm)

RS

WS

To create a smooth join in your binding strips and avoid a lump along the edge of your quilt or project, it is best to join the strips with an angled seam rather than just placing right sides together and stitching a straight seam from edge to edge.

1. Join binding strips by overlapping the end of one strip perpendicular and right sides together with the end of a second strip; you should have an upside-down L shape (fig. 1).

2. Stitch a diagonal seam from the left corner to the right corner of the overlap. Trim the seam allowance to ¼" (0.6cm) with pinking shears, then press the seam allowance open (fig. 2).

If you're not comfortable eyeballing a stitch line, first draw a guideline from corner to corner with a wash-away marker or a light pencil.

Binding Quilt Edges

You can bind projects by folding double-fold bias tape over the raw edges and stitching in one pass, which is typical for making face masks and is the technique used on the Cheery Adult Bib and the Fat Quarter Wheelchair/Walker Caddy. A more traditional quilting technique was used on the edges of the Memory-Care Fidget Mat and Quilt-As-You-Go Lap Blanket. For a doubled binding, I like to cut my strips four times the width of the finished binding, plus ⅛" to ¼" (0.3 to 0.6cm) to accommodate the density of the quilt.

1. Fold the binding strip lengthwise in half. With raw edges aligned, start stitching your binding to the mat/quilt edge, beginning on one side and leaving at least 5" (12.7cm) of unstitched binding as a tail. As you approach the corner, stop stitching ½" (1.3cm) before you reach the edge; so, if your binding is ¼" (0.6cm) wide, stop ¼" (0.6cm) from the edge. Fix your stitching. Fold the binding up at a 90-degree angle (fig. 1).

2. Fold the binding back down so that the raw edge of the binding is flush with the raw edge of the quilt/mat and the top fold is aligned with the original side. Begin stitching where you left off on the previous side, making sure to fix your stitch line at the starting point. Continue around the quilt, stopping approximately 7" to 8" (17.8 to 20.3cm) from your starting point (fig. 2).

3. Place the tails smooth and flat along the quilt edge. The overlap will need to be the same amount as the width of your binding. So, for a 2⅛" (5.4cm) binding, overlay 2⅛" (5.4cm). Clip the excess ends of the tails perpendicular to the edge of the mat (fig. 3).

4. Place the ends right sides together at right angles (refer to Joining Binding Ends on page 22). Stitch a diagonal line from corner to corner and trim off the corner, leaving a ¼" (0.6cm) seam allowance (fig. 4). Now simply finger-press the binding into its original folded shape along the remaining raw edge of the quilt/mat. Press, pin, and continue stitching to secure, fixing your stitch line as you start and stop (fig. 5).

5. Press the binding away from the front edge and fold it over to the back of the quilt/mat. Miter the binding at the corner and hand whipstitch into place with a single thread (fig. 6).

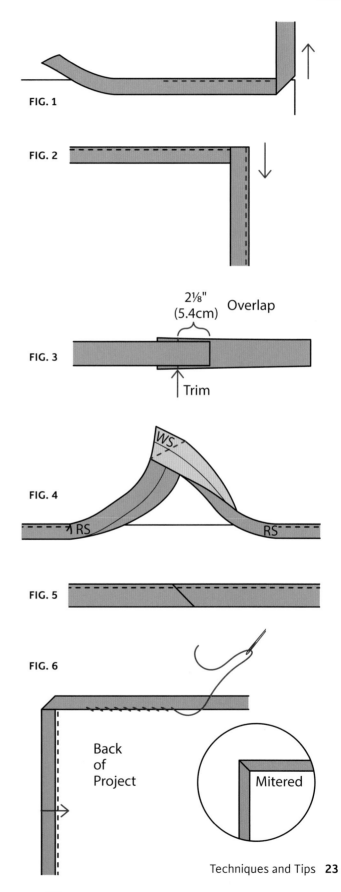

FIG. 1

FIG. 2

2⅛"
(5.4cm) Overlap

FIG. 3

Trim

WS

FIG. 4

RS   RS

FIG. 5

FIG. 6

Back
of
Project

Mitered

PART 2

Projects

It's time to make your first thoughtful health aid gift! Pick whatever project speaks to you or would be appreciated by the lucky recipient you have in mind. Or try your skills at one of the easier projects in the book, like the Cheery Adult Bib or the Pleated Face Mask with Pocket. Don't be afraid to pick out a great fabric print that will speak to the user of the item and then enjoy putting all your warmth and care into your sewing.

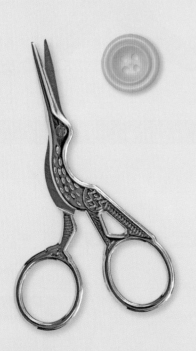

Cheery Adult Bib

In nursing-care facilities across the nation, and in particular in memory-care units, residents often need an extra layer of protection during meals to keep their clothes safe from spills. This adult-size bib is a 1-yard (0.91m) wonder—well, 2 yards (1.83m) if you count the lining—and can be made in any print. Pick a print that might mean something to your loved one. The Velcro closure at the back makes it easy to take on and off, meaning it not only keeps residents neat and tidy but also results in less laundry for caregivers.

MATERIALS

- Cheery Adult Bib pattern pieces: A, B, C, D
- 1 yard (0.91m) of cotton print
- 1 yard (0.91m) of terry cloth
- 3⅓ yards (3.05m) of ½" (1.3cm)–wide double-fold coordinating bias tape
- Velcro Sticky Back for fabrics (permanent), 1" x ¾" (2.5 x 2cm) ovals

TOOLS

- Glass head pins
- Fabric glue pen
- Sewing scissors
- Universal needle
- Thread to match

All seam allowances are ⅜" (1cm) unless otherwise noted.

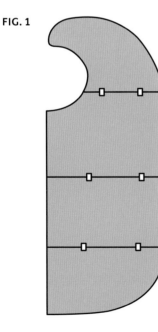

FIG. 1

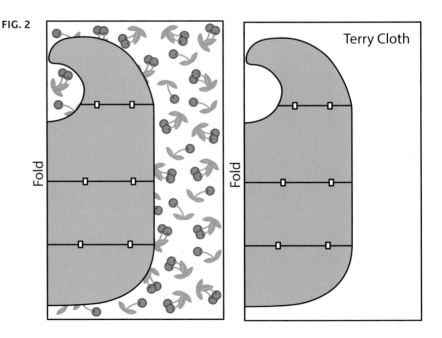

FIG. 2

Terry Cloth

Fold

Fold

1. Join the pattern pieces as indicated to create a complete half pattern (fig. 1).

2. Cut out one bib on the fold from cotton print and one bib on the fold from terry cloth (fig. 2).

Tip

While Velcro is probably the easiest to manipulate quickly, large snaps, or even a button and buttonhole, could be used to secure the bib.

FIG. 3

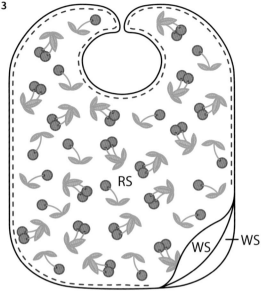

3. Place wrong sides together. Pin all around and stitch with a 3.0 length completely around the bib to secure the layers together (fig. 3).

FIG. 4

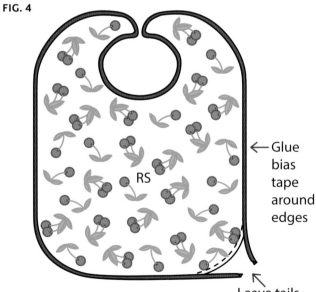

← Glue bias tape around edges

Leave tails

4. The easiest and quickest way to bind the edges of the bib is to use purchased double-fold ½" (1.3cm) bias tape, fold around the edges, and topstitch through all layers. However, if the raw edge of the bib doesn't rest right up against the inside crease of the bias tape, the finish will pucker, and you will have a slight challenge as you ease

the tape around the neck tabs. Here is when a fabric glue pen comes in handy. Start your bias tape in a lower left edge. Leave about 4" (10.2cm) at the start where you do not glue, then slowly glue just inside the bib's raw edge and finger-press your bias tape in place around the edge, making sure the bib's raw edge will rest right up against the bias tape crease (fig. 4).

FIG. 5

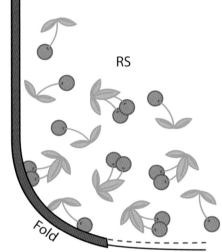

5. Work completely around the bib, easing the tape around the neck tabs, and stop so that you have 5" to 6" (12.7 to 15.2cm) of space where the binding is not glued. Do not cut off the excess bias tape (fig. 5).

FIG. 6

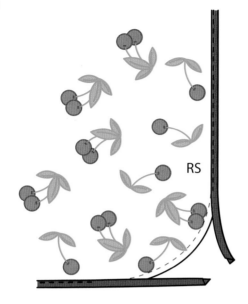

6. Starting where you began the glued portion of the tape, edge stitch around the binding, securing the tape on the front and back. Before stitching all the way around, check to make sure your bobbin line of stitching is catching the bias tape on the back side. If not, move your needle position to the right until it does. Stitch slowly and carefully, stopping where the glued bias tape ends (fig. 6).

7. You could simply fold one short raw edge of your bias tape to the wrong side, overlap that end over the remaining end where the bias tape meets along the edge of the bib, and stitch down to finish. A much cleaner finish can be borrowed from your quilting techniques. Overlap the tails the same amount as the width of your bias tape—in this case, 1½" (3.8cm). Clip the ends of the tails perpendicular to the edge of the bib. Refer to Joining Binding Ends on page 22 to join the ends. Now simply fold the bias tape back into its original position along the remaining raw edge of the bib. Press, glue, and continue stitching to secure, fixing your stitch line as you start and stop.

8. Apply Velcro on the back of the front tab and the front of the back tab, nicely aligned. Make sure to place the soft circles on the cotton half of your bib and the rough circles on the terry cloth. If the rough circles are facing the terry cloth, they can grab the pile and snag it (fig. 7).

FIG. 7

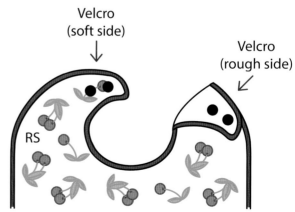

Velcro
(soft side)

Velcro
(rough side)

RS

Half-Hour Ear-Saver Headband

It doesn't take long for the skin at the base of your ears to get irritated from the elastic used to secure a face mask. The first person to come up with the idea of adding buttons to a headband on which to loop the elastic instead was a genius. That wasn't me, but I can take the credit for drafting up an easy headband pattern that takes less than a half an hour to make and less than one fat quarter in fabric! Team it with a matching mask, and it's an adorable and comfortable ensemble.

MATERIALS

- 1 fat quarter of quilting cotton fabric, 18" x 22" (45.7 x 55.9cm)
- 8" (20.3cm) piece of 1" (2.5cm)–wide elastic
- 2 medium-size two-hole buttons

TOOLS

- Tube turner and/or large safety pin
- Universal needle
- Clear ruler
- Seam gauge
- Sewing scissors
- Wash-away marker
- Thread to match

CUTTING LIST

- From fat quarter:
  - 1 strip, 6" x 18" (15.2 x 45.7cm) long
  - 1 strip, 3¼" x 8" (8.3 x 20.3cm) long

All seam allowances are ½" (1.3cm) unless otherwise noted.

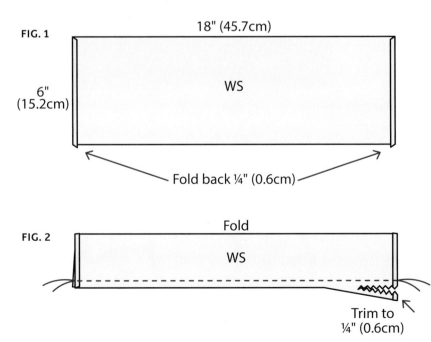

FIG. 1
18" (45.7cm)
WS
6" (15.2cm)
Fold back ¼" (0.6cm)

FIG. 2
Fold
WS
Trim to ¼" (0.6cm)

1. Fold each short end of the 18" (45.7cm) strip ¼" (0.6cm) to the wrong side and press (fig. 1).

2. Fold the 18" (45.7cm) strip in half lengthwise, with raw edges even. Press. Stitch the raw edges together, making sure the ¼" (0.6cm) ends are still turned back; fix your stitching when you start and stop. Trim the seam allowance to ¼" (0.6cm) with pinking shears and press the seam allowance open (fig. 2).

Tip

Check out the project
for the coordinating
mask on page 60.

FIG. 3

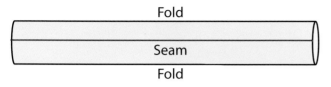

Fold

Seam

Fold

3. Turn the tube right side out. You can use a tube turner, but this piece is relatively wide and turns fairly easily. Press so that the seam will fall in the center back of your headband (fig. 3). Set aside.

4. Press the 8" (20.3cm) strip right sides together without turning under the short raw edges. Stitch up the long raw edge, trim, and press. Turn as you did for the larger strip. For this narrower strip, a tube turner comes in very handy. Once turned, press your seam line to the bottom edge rather than the center back.

FIG. 4

1½"
(3.8cm)

1½"
(3.8cm)

5. Using a large safety pin or your tube turner, insert the 8" (20.3cm) piece of elastic into the 8" (20.3cm) fabric tube and gather up the fabric so that 1½" (3.8cm) of the elastic extends from each open end. Pin the fabric ends to the elastic to secure (fig. 4).

FIG. 5

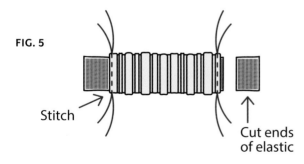

Stitch

Cut ends
of elastic

6. Stitch across each end of the fabric/elastic band a scant ⅛" (0.3cm) from the edge of the fabric to secure. Be sure to adjust the pins as you stitch so the sewing machine needle does not hit them. Once complete, clip off the excess elastic (fig. 5).

½" (1.3cm)

FIG. 6A

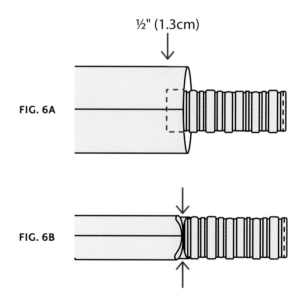

FIG. 6B

7. Place the headband tube on an ironing board or other flat surface. Insert one end of the covered elastic tube ½" (1.3cm) into one open end of the headband tube. Pinch the headband opening so that the sides meet at the center top of the elastic tube and then pin together. Then press the excess headband fabric above the pin flat into a box pleat (see next step) and pin down each side (figs. 6a and 6b).

or secured in a seam to maintain its form. Topstitch approximately ⅛" (0.3cm) from the end of the box pleat through all layers to secure the headband sections together. Fix your stitching at the beginning and end (fig. 7).

9. Repeat steps 7 and 8 on the remaining end.

10. Put the headband on where comfortable. Place your mask over your face and pull the elastic to where it will comfortably loop over a button on each side. Mark the headband with a marking tool and hand or machine stitch a large button where marked. Refer to Attaching Buttons (by machine or hand, as preferred) on page 19 or 20.

> **NOTE:** While many headbands are made from knits or stretch fabrics, these are a not a good choice if you are planning to add buttons to secure a face mask. When made of a knit fabric, the band will stretch, so when you loop the elastic around the buttons, it will pull them forward and won't hold the mask securely. This pattern does work ideally with knits or stretch fabrics if you're wearing it solely as a headband and not to anchor a mask.

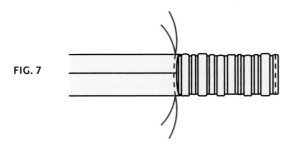

FIG. 7

8. A box pleat is one of the most common types of pleats. It's formed by folding a section of fabric back on itself, then mirror-imaging an identical fold a determined width away so that the folds typically meet evenly at the center back. The top edge of the pleat is topstitched

Ponytail Scrub Cap

Healthcare workers with longer hair love this Ponytail Scrub Cap. The cap works up easily with ½ yard (45.7cm) of fabric, is very roomy, and protects the workers' hair throughout their shifts so it doesn't require everyday washing, which can stress their locks. With an adjustable strap, this cap fits everyone.

MATERIALS

- Ponytail Scrub Cap pattern pieces: Crown A, Crown B
- ½ yard (45.7cm) of 44" (1.12m)–wide quilting cotton
- 4" (10.2cm) square of tear-away stabilizer
- Optional: instead of sewing ties, you can opt for 2 strips of 22" x ⅜" (55.9 x 1cm) ribbon

TOOLS

- Glass head pins
- Seam ripper
- Thread to match
- Sewing scissors
- Seam gauge
- Wash-away marker

CUTTING LIST

- From quilting cotton:
  - 1 square, 17" (43.2cm), for cap
  - 1 rectangle, 39½" x 6½" (100.3 x 16.5cm), for band
  - 1 strip, 44" x 2" (1.12m x 5cm), for ties (if not using ribbon)

FIG. 1

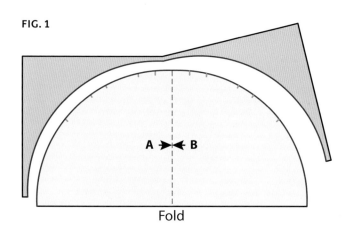

A ►◄ B

Fold

1. Trace off the two quarter patterns, making sure to include all the markings. Tape the two pieces together as instructed. Fold your 17" (43.2cm) square in half lengthwise and press. Pin the pattern on your folded square so the bottom folded edges align with the fold marks on the pattern. Cut out along the curve (fig. 1). Mark the pleat lines on your fabric before removing the pattern with a wash-away marker.

FIG. 2

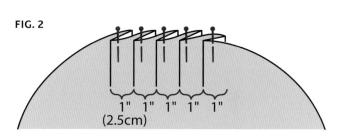

1" 1" 1" 1" 1"
(2.5cm)

2. Fold, press, and pin the five 1" (2.5cm) pleats along the edge of your cap, following the traced marks (fig. 2). Set aside.

FIG. 3

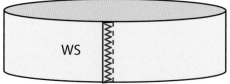

WS

3. With right sides and raw edges together, align the short ends of the band piece and stitch with a ½" (1.3cm) seam allowance (fig. 3). Finish the seam allowance with a zigzag stitch or serger and press to the left.

Tip

Make sure you space your ties in order to pull in enough fullness to fit the head of the medical worker who will be wearing the cap. Baste first, then remove the basted ties and reposition if needed.

FIG. 4

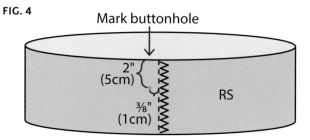

Mark buttonhole

2" (5cm)

3⁄8" (1cm)

RS

4. On the right side of the band, mark a buttonhole 3⁄8" (1cm) to the left of the seam line and 2" (5cm) from the raw edge (fig. 4).

FIG. 5

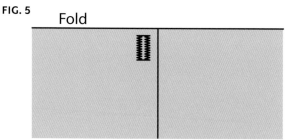

Fold

5. Press under the long raw edge of the band (on the buttonhole side) 3⁄4" (1.9cm). Select a 1" (2.5cm) basic buttonhole, place a rectangle of tear-away stabilizer underneath the area to be stitched, and stitch your buttonhole, starting at your mark from the previous step. Carefully tear away the stabilizer (fig. 5).

FIG. 6

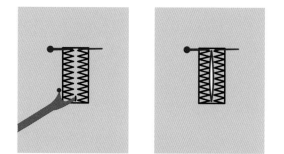

6. Place a pin horizontally just below the horizontal stitching at the top of the buttonhole. Insert a seam ripper just inside the bottommost thread and carefully run it up the center of the buttonhole, ending at the pin. The pin will keep the seam ripper from cutting though the threads at the top of the buttonhole (fig. 6).

FIG. 7

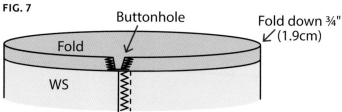

Buttonhole

Fold down 3⁄4" (1.9cm)

Fold

WS

7. Still working on the buttonhole side, fold the long edge of the band to the wrong side 3⁄4" (1.9cm) again to create your tie casing. The buttonhole will be at the edge of the fold (fig. 7). You will not stitch the casing closed yet.

FIG. 8

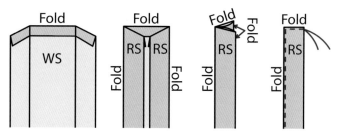

Fold / WS / Fold / RS RS / Fold / Fold / RS / Fold / Fold / RS

8. Fold the short ends of the tie strip to the wrong side 1⁄4" (0.6cm) and press. Press lengthwise in half, wrong sides together, to crease the strip. Unfold, then fold the long edges of the tie strip to the wrong side 1⁄2" (1.3cm) to meet evenly at the center crease. Press. Fold the strip in half again to create a 1⁄2" (1.3cm) strip and press. Edge stitch across one short folded-under end and down the long (open) edge, then across the opposite short end, securing your stitching when you start and stop. Cut the strip in half (fig. 8).

FIG. 9

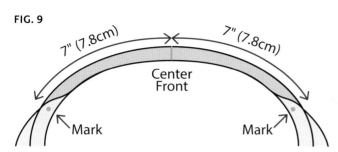

9. Fold the band to find the center front. (The seam is the center back.) Measure 7" (17.8cm) to either side of the center front and, using a wash-away marker, make a mark inside the casing (fig. 9).

FIG. 10

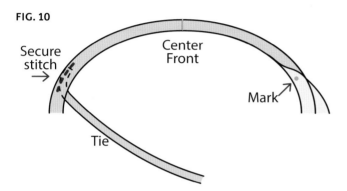

10. Position one raw edge of a tie over a mark, nestled in the fold of the casing with the finished edge of the tie extending to the back. Pin. Fold the casing back over the tie and stitch horizontally through all layers, anchoring the tie (fig. 10). Repeat for the remaining tie on the opposite side of the band.

FIG. 11

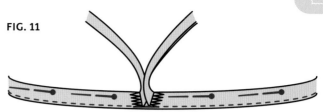

11. Insert the ends of the ties from the inside of the cap out of the buttonhole and pin them smoothly along the fold of the casing. You will be edge stitching the casing all the way around, so make sure the ties are against the inside fold. Edge stitch all the way around the casing. Tug on your ties to make sure they pull out and haven't been caught in the edge stitching (fig. 11).

FIG. 12

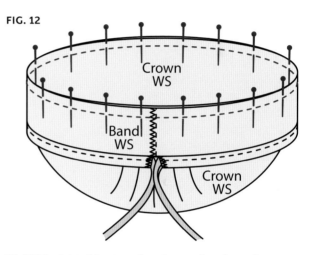

12. With right sides together, insert the pleated crown inside the band, positioning the center pleat at the center back seam and the raw edges even. Pin all the way around, adjusting the pleats to fit the band if needed (fig. 12).

FIG. 13

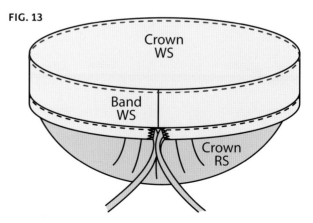

13. Stitch around the crown with a ½" (1.3cm) seam allowance and finish with a zigzag or serger (fig. 13).

Tab Blankie

One of the sweetest and easiest projects you can make for a little one is a tab blankie, and it is surprisingly soothing. Older babies will often pick a favorite colored tab and use their little fingers to rub the texture or poke through the loops. The small size makes a tab blankie easy to transport or store in a hospital environment. You can even choose to loop a tag around a teething toy and stitch it in place. The key is making sure the tags are stitched in securely so that the blankie is safe to use and lasts a long time.

MATERIALS

- ○ ½ yard (45.7cm) each of two different coordinating fleece or Minky fabrics
- ○ 15" (38.1cm) of eight different ribbons (select a variety of different colors, patterns, and textures)

TOOLS

- ○ Universal or ballpoint needle
- ○ Sewing scissors
- ○ Glass head pins
- ○ Thread to match fleece for bottom and top thread
- ○ Seam gauge

CUTTING LIST

- ○ From fleece or Minky:
  - ○ 1 square, 15" (38.1cm), from each fabric
- ○ From ribbons:
  - ○ 3 strips, 4½" (11.4cm) long, from each of eight ribbons

FIG. 1

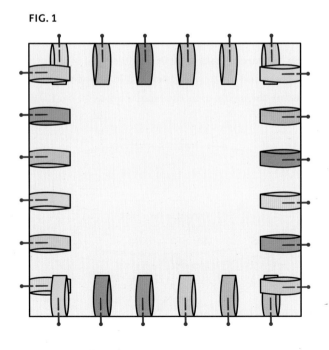

1. Select one of your fleece squares and place it right side up on a flat surface. Starting and stopping 1½" to 2" (3.8 to 5cm) from each corner, position six tabs in a pleasing arrangement, equal distances apart, on each side of the square. (A seam gauge is very helpful for measuring placement.) One at a time, fold a ribbon strip in half to create a tab and pin it in place with the raw edges even to the raw edge of the fleece square. Repeat with each tab, making sure they are spaced evenly (fig. 1).

DISCLAIMER: Even if your blankie is just for family use, you need to make sure it is safely constructed. Refer to the United States Consumer Products Safety Commission guidance on Small Parts for Toys and Children's Projects (www.cpsc.gov/Business--Manufacturing/Business-Education/Business-Guidance/Small-Parts-for-Toys-and-Childrens-Products).

Tip

Pick trims and ribbons in all sorts of different textures and in colors that little ones love. Just make sure you never use a wire-edged trim.

FIG. 2

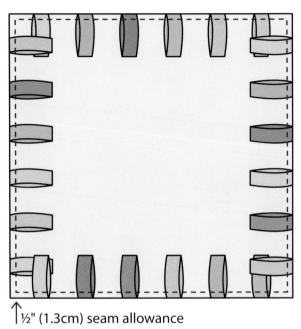

↑ ½" (1.3cm) seam allowance

2. Using a ½" (1.3cm) seam allowance, stitch around the square to secure the tabs, removing the pins as you go (fig. 2).

3. Place your second fleece square right side down over your tab square. Check to see that the squares align. If not, square up to the same size using a straight edge. Pin the layers together completely around.

4. Start midway up on the left side of the pinned square and, using a ⅝" (1.6cm) seam allowance, begin stitching around the square. Make sure to fix or backstitch the beginning of your stitch line to secure the stitches. Stop stitching one to two stitches before you plan to pivot at the first corner and instead stitch an angled one or two stitches across the corner and continue stitching around, repeating this same technique at each corner. This helps create a sharper point when the blankie is turned right side out. Stop stitching approximately 5" (12.7cm) before your starting point and backstitch or fix the end of your stitch line. You need to leave an opening for turning (fig. 3).

FIG. 3

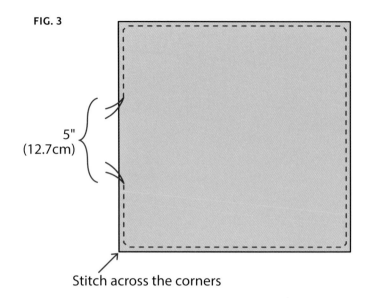

5"
(12.7cm)

Stitch across the corners

5. Trim across all four corners a scant ⅛" (0.3cm) beyond the angled stitch line. Fleece does not fray, so you can trim relatively closely; just make sure not to clip the stitch line. Turn the blankie right side out through the opening in your stitch line.

6. Finger-press all the way around and, if desired, press using a pressing cloth or towel so as not to crush the surface of your fleece.

FIG. 4

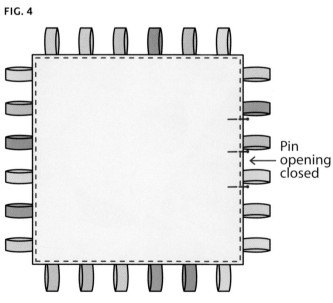

Pin
opening
closed

7. Flip under the seam allowance at the opening and pin or glue closed (fig. 4). Topstitch ¼" (0.6cm) from the raw edges all the way around the square, making sure to secure your stitching.

Tip

Use coordinating colors on both front and back to match the color scheme of the child's room.

Stretch Knit Face Covering/Scarf

Looking for a comfortable face covering that offers an added element of style? Look no further. This easy-to-make design takes just an hour plus prep time and wears like a style-savvy scarf (with elastic tucked under); just pull up as needed. Lyocell spandex or rayon spandex blends seem to work best with this design, and there is no need for a nosepiece due to the stretch.

MATERIALS

- Stretch Knit Face Covering/Scarf pattern pieces: A, B
- ⅜ yard (34cm) of cotton/Lycra knit (knit shown is 97% cotton/3% Lycra)
- 10" (25.4cm) of ¼" (0.6cm)–wide flat elastic
- Optional: ⅜ yard (34cm) of tricot fusible interfacing

TOOLS

- Ballpoint needle
- Sewing scissors
- Thread to match
- Wash-away marker
- Optional: EZ-Steam™ II fusible tape

All seam allowances are ¼" (0.6cm) unless otherwise noted.

FIG. 1

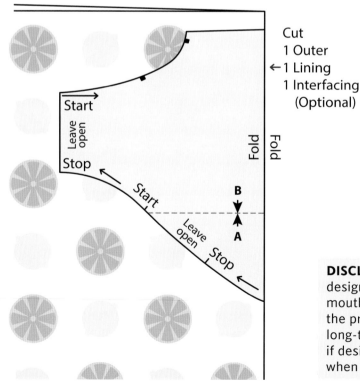

Cut
1 Outer
← 1 Lining
1 Interfacing
(Optional)

Start

Leave open

Stop

Fold

Fold

Start

Leave open

Stop

B

A

1. Cut out one outer mask and one lining mask on the fold of your knit fabric using the pattern. Mark the elastic placement and where to start and stop stitching with a wash-away marker. Optional: If you want an extra layer of protection, cut out one pattern from your tricot fusible interfacing. If your interfacing only has two-way stretch, your stretch needs to be crosswise. Fuse your interfacing to the mask lining (fig. 1).

DISCLAIMER: Interfacing products are not designed for long-term use around the nose/mouth and their manufacturers have not tested the products for potentially toxic effects from long-term use. Include interfacing in your mask if desired at your own risk, or feel free to omit when creating this project.

FIG. 4

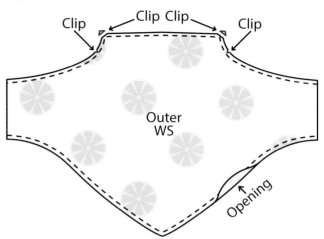

FIG. 2

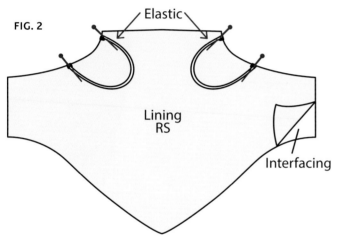

2. Cut your 10" (25.4cm) strip of elastic into two 5" (12.7cm) pieces and pin to the marks on the right side of your lining mask as shown (fig. 2).

4. Using a zigzag stitch with a length of 1.5 and width of 0.5, stitch around the mask at the starting and stopping points. Stitch back and forth at least twice where the elastic is pinned for reinforcement. Do not stitch the short sides (both need to remain open); backstitch in those areas to secure your stitching. Note that when stitching knit fabric, engage your dual feed, if available, on your sewing machine. If you don't have that option, be careful not to stretch the knit as you stitch. Clip across the top corners and clip into the seam allowance at an angle as shown (fig. 4).

FIG. 3

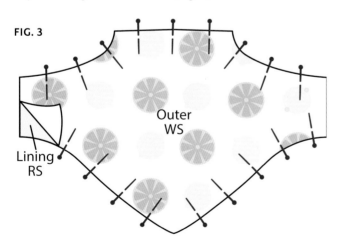

3. Place your outer mask right sides together with the lining mask, sandwiching the elastic (fig. 3).

FIG. 5

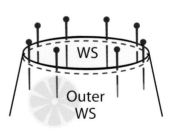

5. Through the opening in your stitch line, reach in and push the left side opening into the right side opening, wrong sides together, with seam allowances open and matching so you have a doubled circle. Pin, making sure the seams are aligned, and stitch around the circle using the same slight zigzag settings (fig. 5).

FIG. 6A

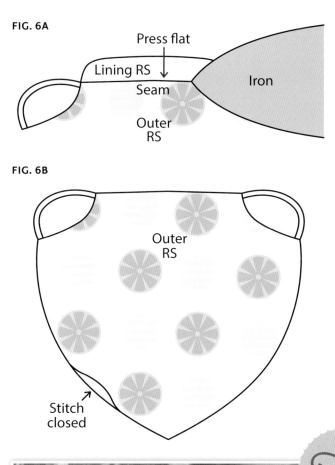

Press flat

Lining RS

Seam

Outer RS

Iron

FIG. 6B

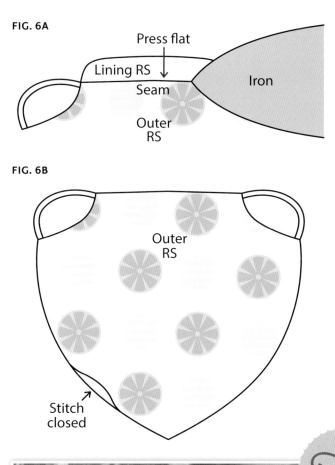

Outer RS

Stitch closed

6. Turn the mask right side out through the opening. Press around the edges, pressing the seams flat first (fig. 6a). Now press so the seam line is right at the edge of the mask all the way around, turning under the opening edges ¼" (0.6cm). Hand stitch the opening closed. You can edge stitch with a slight zigzag if preferred (fig. 6b). Optional: Cut a length of EZ-Steam™ II fusible tape as long as your opening. Finger-press the sticky side to the lining side of your opening so that the edge of the tape is where you would want your seam line to be. Gently peel off the paper backing and finger-press the mask side to the tape, aligning the lining and mask edges. Cover with a slightly damp pressing cloth and press down firmly with an iron on a cotton setting for about ten to twenty seconds.

7. To wear, just pull over your head and adjust the elastic under the fold while the piece is around your neck like a scarf, then pull up and fasten the elastic over your ears to turn it into a mask.

Tip This unisex design wears well, washes well, and can be reversed and worn with the print or solid side facing out.

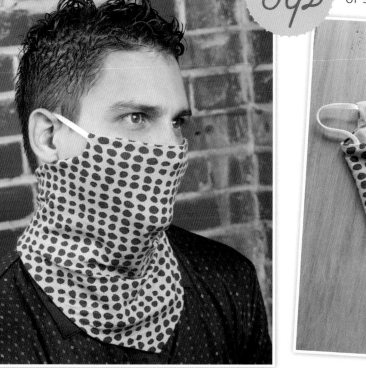

Fat Quarter Scrub Cap

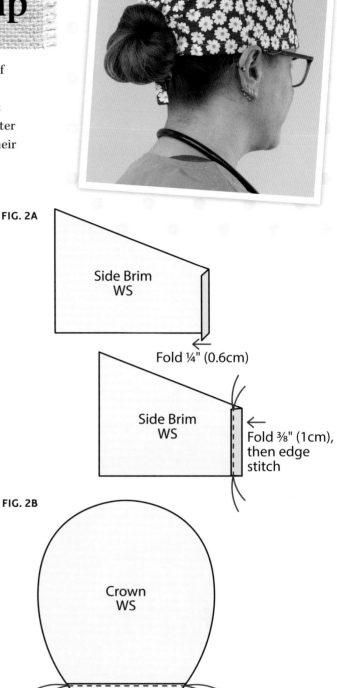

Sew up a scrub cap quickly and easily with a minimal amount of fabric. If you are anything like me, you won't even have to shop for fabric, because you have a stash of cute fat quarters you just couldn't say no to during previous shopping trips. The Fat Quarter Scrub Cap is perfect for medical personnel who need to keep their hair covered and protected during their long shifts and is more fitted than the Ponytail Scrub Cap.

MATERIALS

- Fat Quarter Scrub Cap pattern pieces: Crown, Ties, Front Brim, Side Brim
- 1 fat quarter of quilting cotton fabric, 18" x 22" (45.7 x 55.9cm)
- Optional: 4" (10.2cm)–long piece of ⅛" (0.3cm)–wide elastic

TOOLS

- Sewing scissors
- Small safety pin
- Glass head pins
- Seam ripper
- Thread to match
- Seam gauge
- Wash-away marker

FIG. 2A

Side Brim
WS

Fold ¼" (0.6cm)

Side Brim
WS

Fold ⅜" (1cm), then edge stitch

FIG. 1

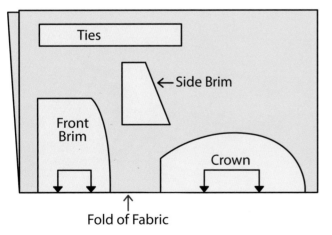

Ties

← Side Brim

Front Brim

Crown

Fold of Fabric

FIG. 2B

Crown
WS

Fold   Edge stitch

1. Trace the pattern pieces, making sure to include all markings. Lay out your pattern pieces and pin them on your folded fat quarter as shown (fig. 1).

2. Fold the short ends of the side brim under ¼" (0.6cm), press, and then fold again ⅜" (1cm). Press and edge stitch across. Repeat for the second side brim (fig. 2a). Repeat these same steps for the bottom straight edge of the crown (fig. 2b).

This style is so cute if you have a ponytail that doesn't need to be covered. Just position your ponytail so the opening in the back ties perfectly around it (see photo on page 46).

FIG. 3A

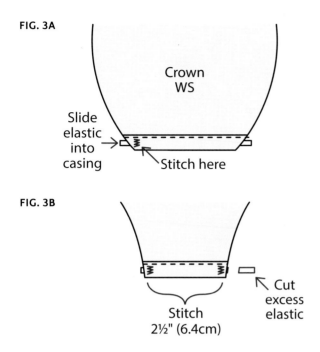

Slide elastic into casing

Crown WS

Stitch here

FIG. 3B

Cut excess elastic

Stitch 2½" (6.4cm)

3. Slide the elastic into the casing at the bottom of the crown. If it is easier, you can attach a safety pin to the end of the elastic to feed it through the casing and simply remove it afterward. Zigzag stitch over one end of the casing to secure the elastic on that end (fig. 3a). Pull the elastic snugly from the free end until the bottom of your casing measures 2½" (6.4cm). Zigzag stitch the elastic securely on this end through all layers of the casing and then clip the excess elastic on each end (fig. 3b). Note: The elastic is optional; you can choose to leave it out completely.

FIG. 4

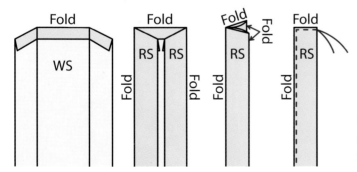

Fold

WS

Fold

RS | RS

Fold

Fold

RS

Fold

Fold

Fold

RS

Fold

4. Fold one short end of the tie strip to the wrong side ¼" (0.6cm) and press. Press lengthwise in half, wrong sides together, to crease the strip. Unfold, then fold the long edges of the tie strip to the wrong side ¼" (0.6cm) to meet evenly at the center crease. Press. Fold the strip in half again to create a ½" (1.3cm) strip and press. Edge stitch across the short folded-under end and down the long (open) edge (fig. 4).

FIG. 5

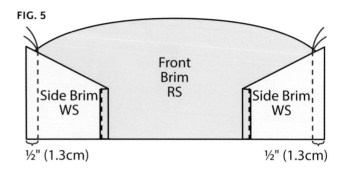

Front Brim RS

Side Brim WS

Side Brim WS

½" (1.3cm)

½" (1.3cm)

5. With right sides and raw edges together, lay the side brim piece on top of the short side edge of the front brim piece. Using a ½" (1.3cm) seam allowance, stitch the side brim onto the front brim. Zigzag or serge the excess seam allowance. Press the seam allowance to the outside. Repeat with the side brim on the opposite side (fig. 5).

FIG. 6

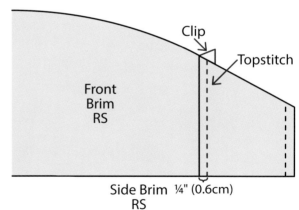

Clip

Topstitch

Front Brim RS

Side Brim ¼" (0.6cm) RS

6. On the right side, topstitch ¼" (0.6cm) away from the seam where you joined the side brim, being sure to catch the excess seam allowance on the back side within that stitch. This step is optional, but I like the way it gives the hat a finished look. Repeat with the opposite side. Clip the small excess flap sticking above the top of the brim on each side (fig. 6).

FIG. 7

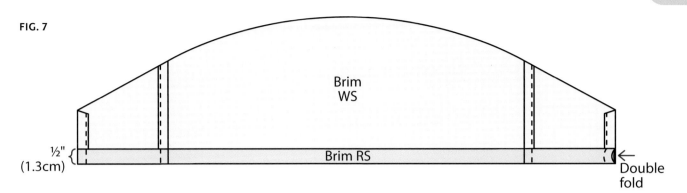

½"
(1.3cm)

Brim WS

Brim RS

← Double fold

7. Fold the long straight edge of the brim up 1" (2.5cm) toward the wrong side of the fabric and press. Fold the raw edge under ½" (1.3cm) and press (fig. 7).

FIG. 8

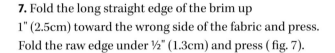

Front Middle of Brim →

Brim WS

Secure tie inside casing fold

Edge stitch →

½"
(1.3cm)

8. Sandwich the unfinished end of the hat tie between the fold you just made and the wrong side of the fabric. The tie will extend into your fold from the side by ½" (1.3cm). Pin it, then stitch it on securely by sewing a small square or a tight zigzag stitch just at the end. Repeat for the opposite side (fig. 8), then edge stitch along the top edge of the bottom casing from one side to the other.

FIG. 9

Align middle center of crown with brim

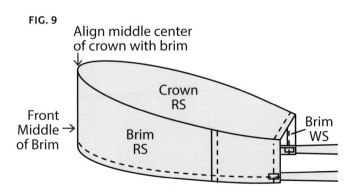

Crown RS

Front Middle of Brim →

Brim RS

Brim WS

9. With right sides and raw edges together, align the middle top of the crown with the middle top of the brim (fig. 9).

FIG. 10

Align middle center of crown with brim

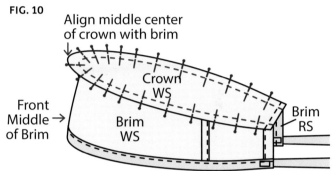

Crown WS

Front Middle of Brim →

Brim WS

Brim RS

10. Pin the crown to the brim all the way around. Using a ⅜" (1cm) seam allowance, stitch the crown to the brim (fig. 10). Zigzag or serge the edges, then press the seam allowance down toward the brim.

FIG. 11

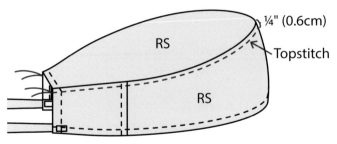

¼" (0.6cm)

RS

Topstitch

RS

11. Press the seam allowance of the crown down toward the brim. Topstitch the brim ¼" (0.6cm) down from the crown seam all the way around, being sure to catch the excess seam allowance in the stitch for a more finished look (fig. 11).

Cooper Unisex Scrub Cap

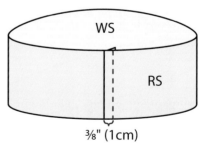

Frontline workers in healthcare won't have to worry about their hair not being fully protected with this scrub hat. It's suitable for both men and women. There are also no concerns about hard-to-find elastics either, because this pattern utilizes any kind of ties, even shoelaces. The back of it differs from a standard unisex cap in that there is no opening, and the ties are inside the casing and act as a cinch-able drawstring to tighten the cap to fit any size head.

MATERIALS

- Cooper Unisex Scrub Cap pattern pieces: Back Brim A, Front Brim B, Crown
- ¼ yard (23cm) of 44" (1.12m)–wide quilting cotton
- 2 ribbons/ties, 18" (45.7cm) in length, or a 1 yard (0.91m) shoelace, cut in half
- 2 squares of 2" (5.1cm)–wide tear-away stabilizer

TOOLS

- Glass head pins
- Seam ripper
- Thread to match
- Sewing scissors
- Seam gauge
- Wash-away marker
- Machine buttonhole foot/attachment

FIG. 1

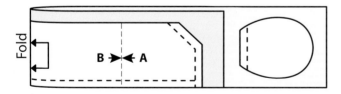

1. Trace the patterns, making sure to include all the markings. Cut out and tape the two brim pattern pieces together as instructed on the pattern pieces. Fold the fabric over enough to accommodate the taped brim pattern, leaving a single layer long enough to fit the crown pattern (fig. 1). Pin the patterns onto the fabric, making sure the front edge of the brim aligns with the folded edge of the fabric. Cut out and transfer all markings with a wash-away marker.

FIG. 2

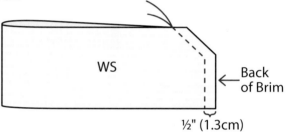

2. With right sides and raw edges together, align the short ends of the brim, then stitch with a ½" (1.3cm) seam allowance (fig. 2). Finish the seam allowance with a serger or zigzag stitch and press to the left.

FIG. 3

3. Topstitch the back of the brim ⅜" (1cm) away from the seam, being certain to catch the seam allowance within this stitch (fig 3).

Tip

Although a more fitted design, this cap still has enough room for tucking longer hair up in the back; plus, the adjustable aspect lets you choose to wear it over or tucked behind your ears.

FIG. 4

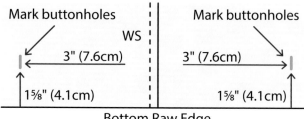

Mark buttonholes WS Mark buttonholes

3" (7.6cm) 3" (7.6cm)

1⅝" (4.1cm) 1⅝" (4.1cm)

Bottom Raw Edge

4. Mark the spots for two buttonholes 1⅝" (4.1cm) above the raw edge and 3" (7.6cm) from the back seam on each side (fig. 4).

FIG. 5

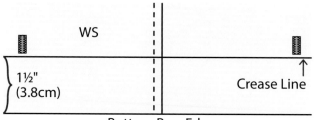

WS

1½" (3.8cm) Crease Line

Bottom Raw Edge

5. Press under the long raw edge of the brim 1½" (3.8cm) all around to form a crease line. The buttonholes are above that crease line. Take the brim to the machine and select a ⅝" (1.6cm)–long buttonhole. Place a small rectangle of tear-away stabilizer under each area to be sewn, then stitch your buttonholes, starting at your marks from the previous step. Upon completion, carefully tear away the stabilizer (fig. 5).

FIG. 6

6. Place a pin horizontally just below the horizontal stitching at the top of the buttonhole. Insert a seam ripper just above the bottom thread and carefully run it up the center of the buttonhole, ending at the pin. This step assures that the seam ripper does not accidentally cut your top threads. Repeat this step with the second buttonhole (fig. 6).

FIG. 7

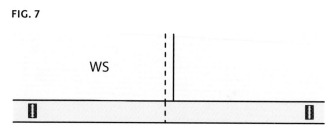

WS

7. Fold the long raw bottom edge of the brim up again to meet the hemline crease you pressed in step 5. Press it all the way around to create the casing. The buttonholes will be inside the casing (fig. 7).

FIG. 8

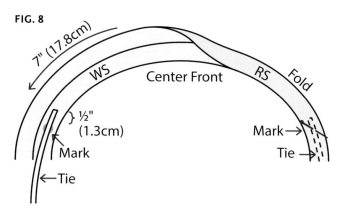

7" (17.8cm) WS Center Front RS Fold

½" (1.3cm) Mark Tie

Mark

←Tie

8. Mark the casing 7" (17.8cm) from the middle front of the brim on each side. Place the cut end of a ribbon or shoelace at the spot you just marked on each side. The cut end will extend past this mark by ½" (1.3cm). The longer end of the tie will face toward the back of the hat. Fold the casing over the cut end of the tie and secure with a pin (fig. 8).

FIG. 9

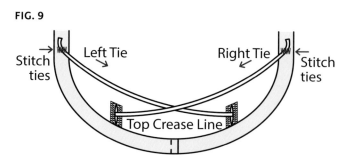

Stitch ties Left Tie Right Tie Stitch ties

Top Crease Line

9. Stitch a line vertically through all layers of the casing, anchoring the tie. Repeat for the other side. Insert the end of the tie from the right side of the brim through the left buttonhole. Insert the tie from the left side of the brim through the right buttonhole. The ties will cross each other (fig. 9).

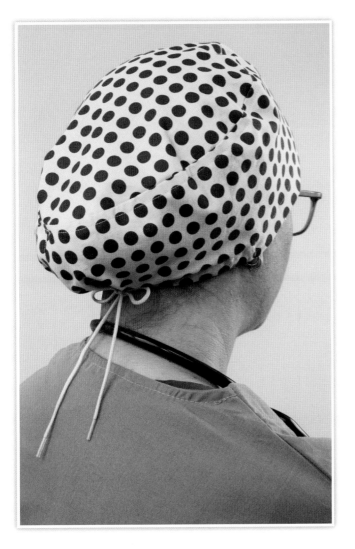

FIG. 11

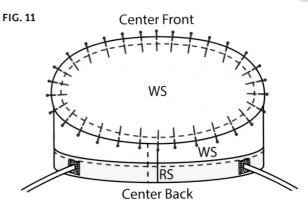

11. With right sides and raw edges together, insert the crown inside the brim by positioning the center front of the crown to the center front of the brim, and the center back of the crown to the back seam of the brim. Pin all the way around. Stitch the crown to the brim using a ⅜" (1cm) seam allowance. Finish with a serger or zigzag stitch (fig. 11).

FIG. 12

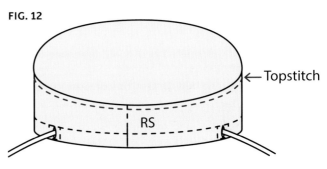

12. Press the seam allowance of the crown down toward the brim. Topstitch ¼" (0.6cm) down from the seam that joins the crown to the brim, all the way around the hat (fig. 12).

FIG. 10

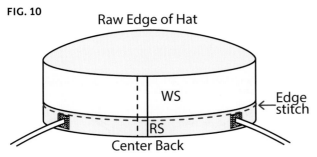

10. Refold any casing that has come unfolded, then nestle the ties into the inside fold of the casing and pin so that you do not accidentally sew over them when you stitch the casing closed. Edge stitch the casing all the way around the brim. When finished, tug on the ties to make sure they pull out and haven't gotten caught in the stitching (fig. 10).

Pleated Face Mask with Pocket

The pleated face mask is probably the easiest to construct of all the standard face masks out there. This particular design has an opening for inserting a filter if desired. The mask can be made with or without a metal nosepiece, and you can choose between elastic ear loops or fabric ties. The fabric tie option, shown at right, allows for maximum adaptability and comfort.

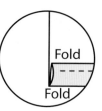

MATERIALS

- Rectangle of woven cotton print or quilting cotton for outer mask of desired size:
  - Standard size: 9½" x 7½" (24.1 x 19.1cm)
  - Large size: 10½" x 8¼" (26.7 x 21cm)
- Optional: Rectangle of lightweight iron-on interfacing of desired size:
  - Standard size: 9½" x 7½" (24.1 x 19.1cm)
  - Large size: 10½" x 8¼" (26.7 x 21cm)
- Rectangle of lightweight flannel or quilting cotton for lining of desired size:
  - Standard size: 14½" x 5¼" (37 x 13.3cm)
  - Large size: 17" x 5½" (43.2 x 14cm)
- 12" (30.5cm) piece of ¼" (0.6cm)–wide elastic, or 2 yards (1.83m) of ½" (1.3cm)–wide double-fold bias tape
- Metal nosepiece (purchased or fashioned from aluminum pan; see page 63)
- 3" (7.6cm) strip of ½" (1.3cm)–wide single-fold bias tape

TOOLS

- Universal needle
- Sewing scissors
- Wash-away marker
- Thread to match

DISCLAIMER: Interfacing products are not designed for long-term use around the nose/ mouth and their manufacturers have not tested the products for potentially toxic effects from long-term use. Include interfacing in your mask if desired at your own risk, or feel free to omit when creating this project.

FIG. 1

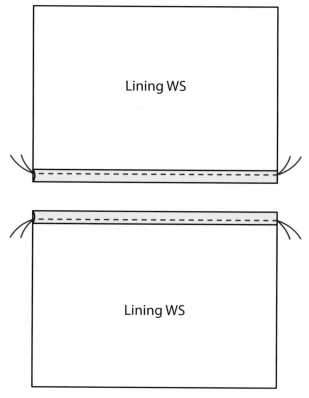

1. Cut the lining fabric rectangle into two equal rectangles, depending on your chosen mask size: either 7¼" x 5¼" (18.4 x 13.3cm) or 8½" x 5½" (21.6 x 14cm). On one long side of each rectangle, turn under ¼" (0.6cm) and press, then turn under ⅜" (1cm) and press. Stitch with a ¼" (0.6cm) seam allowance to secure (fig. 1). If you are not adding a metal nosepiece, skip to step 4.

Tip

Line the interior of your mask with a soft, lightweight flannel for comfort next to your skin as well as breathability and easy care.

FIG. 2

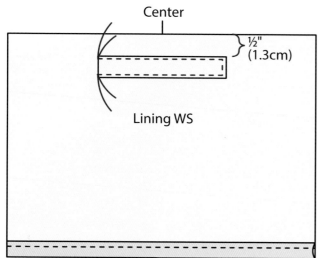

Center

½"
(1.3cm)

Lining WS

2. Optional: Fold one of the lining rectangles from step 1 in half, raw side to raw side, then press to mark the center and unfold. Repeat to find the center of a 3" (7.6cm) strip of single-fold ½" (1.3cm) bias tape. Align the fold of the bias tape with the fold of the fabric rectangle ½" (1.3cm) from the raw upper edge on the wrong side. Pin. Machine stitch around three sides of the bias just a few threads inside the edge, leaving one short end open (fig. 2).

FIG. 3

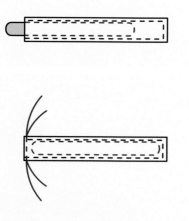

3. Optional: Insert the metal nosepiece into the casing, making sure it is completely inserted and that at least ⅛" (0.3cm) of the bias tape can be stitched down at the open end. If not, trim the nosepiece and re-insert. Stitch across the open end of the bias tape, securing the nosepiece in the casing (fig. 3).

FIG. 4

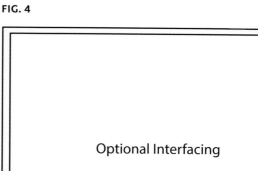

Optional Interfacing

4. Interfacing is optional. Trim ¼" (0.6cm) from all four sides of the interfacing. Center and fuse the interfacing onto the wrong side of the outer mask rectangle. Do not move the iron; use a pressing motion (fig. 4).

FIG. 5

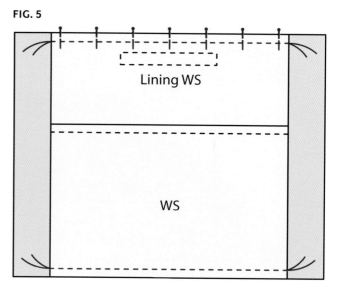

Lining WS

WS

5. Mark the centers of both the lining pieces and the outer mask pieces. With right sides together, place the upper lining rectangle with the nosepiece on the upper edge of the outer mask rectangle, raw edges even and centers aligned. You will have outer mask fabric extending on each side. Pin. Repeat, placing the remaining lining rectangle on the outer mask with the lower raw edges aligned. The lining pieces will overlap in the center. Pin. Stitch across the top and bottom with a ⅜" (1cm) seam to attach the lining pieces (fig. 5).

FIG. 6

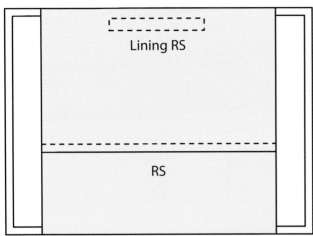

Lining RS

RS

6. Press the seams flat first, then flip the lining pieces so they are wrong sides together with the outer mask rectangle. Press the seams at the top and bottom edges. Overlap the top lining piece over the bottom lining piece (fig. 6).

FIG. 7

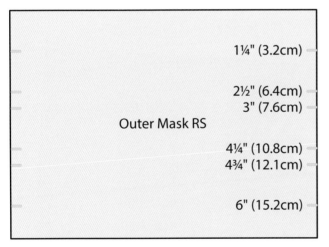

1¼" (3.2cm)

2½" (6.4cm)
3" (7.6cm)

Outer Mask RS

4¼" (10.8cm)
4¾" (12.1cm)

6" (15.2cm)

7. On a flat surface, with the outer mask right side up, mark the fold lines on each side (fig. 7). For a standard mask, make marks from the top edge at 1¼", 2½", 3", 4¼", 4¾", and 6" (3.2, 6.4, 7.6, 10.8, 12.1, and 15.2cm). For a large mask, make marks from the top edge at 1½", 3", 3¾", 5", 5¾", and 7" (3.8, 7.6, 9.5, 12.7, 14.6, and 17.8cm).

FIG. 8

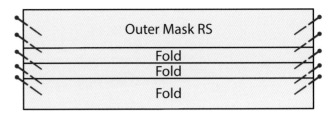

Outer Mask RS
Fold
Fold
Fold

8. Fold in the pleats on both sides, with the first mark meeting the second mark, the third meeting the fourth, and the fifth meeting the sixth. Press and pin to secure. Make sure the lining has been pinched and folded neatly in with the outer mask. The large mask should measure approximately 3¼" (8.3cm) and the standard mask approximately 3" (7.6cm) on the pleated edges (fig. 8).

FIG. 9

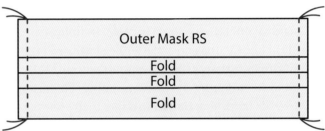

Outer Mask RS
Fold
Fold
Fold

9. Stitch to secure the pleats with a ⅜" (1cm) seam on each side (fig. 9). From here, you can choose to finish with elastic ear loops or fabric ties.

To Add Elastic Ear Loops

FIG. 10

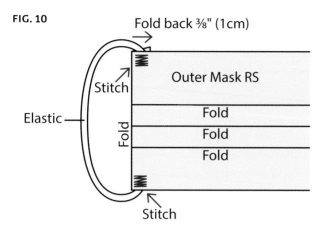

FIG. 11

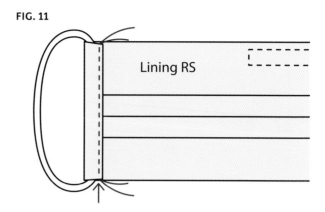

1. Fold down the pleated ends along the ⅜" (1cm) seam line and press. Cut a 6" (15.2cm) piece of ¼" (0.6cm)–wide elastic and place underneath the fold, overlapping the end of the elastic over the mask edge by approximately ¼" (0.6cm). Stitch across the fabric fold, securing the elastic in place. Zigzag or straight stitch back and forth several times to ensure the elastic won't pull out (fig. 10).

2. Loop the remaining end of the elastic to the adjacent side of the fold and repeat.

3. Press under the fold with the elastic attached ½" (1.3cm), making sure the fold back overlaps the raw edge of the lining. Pin if needed, and secure with a ⅜" (1cm) seam, being careful not to catch the elastic loop in your stitching. Repeat to secure the elastic on the opposite side of the mask (fig. 11).

To Add Ear Ties

FIG. 12

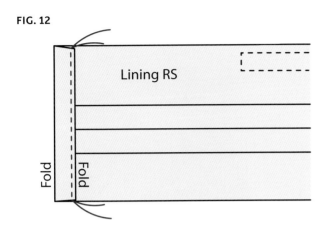

1. Fold back the pleated ends along the ⅜" (1cm) seam line and press. Fold another ½" (1.3cm) and press, making sure the fold back overlaps the raw edge of the lining. Pin if needed, and stitch to secure the fold back. Repeat on the opposite side of the mask (fig. 12).

FIG. 13

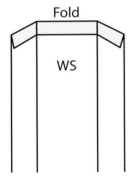

2. Cut two 32" to 34" (81.3 to 86.4cm) strips of ½" (1.3cm) double-fold bias tape. Press in half lengthwise to find the strip center. Open up the short ends of the bias tape and turn the raw edges ¼" (0.6cm) to the inside and press (fig. 13).

FIG. 14

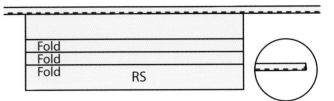

3. Measure and mark the center of the mask. Unfold the bias tape and place the mask inside, aligning the mask center with the bias tape center and making sure the top raw edge of the mask is against the inside fold of the bias tape. Pin or use fabric glue to secure the bias tape in place. Refold the bias tape edges down the complete length. Glue if you feel more comfortable keeping them aligned while you stitch, and make sure the ends are turned under to create a finished edge (fig. 14).

FIG. 15

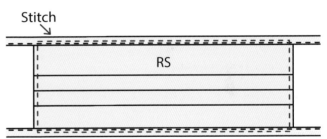

4. Edge stitch the bias tape to the mask by starting at one mask side and sewing through all layers. At ⅛" (0.3cm) from the tie end, pivot and stitch across the end. Backstitch to secure. Return to the side of the mask where you started stitching and sew the remaining side of the tie. Add the second strip of bias tape to the bottom of the mask, following steps 3 and 4 again (fig. 15).

When stitching across the end of a narrow tie, it will often bunch up under your presser foot. To avoid this, stop your stitching about 2" (5cm) before the end, place a 3" (7.6cm) square of light tear-away stabilizer underneath that section, then continue stitching to the end. When finished, carefully tear away the stabilizer so as not to pull out your stitching.

Shaped Face Mask

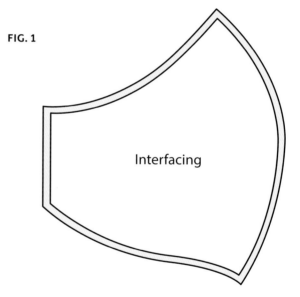

Fit is very important when wearing a face mask, and this design, with a curve to the lower edge, has proven to provide a superior fit. The most important step in construction is making sure you securely fix your stitching at the sides of the mask before turning right sides out, as the opening is slightly smaller than other designs, meaning that turning puts added stress on those stitches.

MATERIALS

- Shaped Face Mask pattern piece
- 18" x 9" (45.7 x 22.9cm) rectangle of quilter's cotton
- 18" x 9" (45.7 x 22.9cm) rectangle of soft flannel
- Optional: 18" x 9" (45.7 x 22.9cm) rectangle of medium-weight to heavyweight fusible interfacing
- Metal nosepiece (or rectangle cut from aluminum pan; see page 63)
- Two 6" to 6½" (15.2 to 16.5cm) lengths of narrow flat or round elastic no wider than ¼" (0.6cm)
- 3" (7.6cm) piece of ½" (1.3cm)–wide single-fold bias tape

TOOLS

- Universal needle
- Sewing scissors
- Glass head pins

CUTTING LIST

- Cut two masks (right and left side) from quilter's cotton, flannel, and interfacing using the mask pattern.

All seam allowances are ¼" (0.6cm) unless otherwise noted.

FIG. 1

Interfacing

1. Interfacing is optional. Trim away a scant ¼" (0.6cm) around all four edges of your interfacing mask pieces. Fuse to the quilter's cotton mask pieces (outer mask) following the manufacturer's instructions (fig. 1).

DISCLAIMER: Interfacing products are not designed for long-term use around the nose/mouth and their manufacturers have not tested the products for potentially toxic effects from long-term use. Include interfacing in your mask if desired at your own risk, or feel free to omit when creating this project.

Tip

If using round elastic cord rather than flat elastic on a face mask, always tie a knot at each end that will rest beyond the stitch line so the elastic does not pull out when it's stretched.

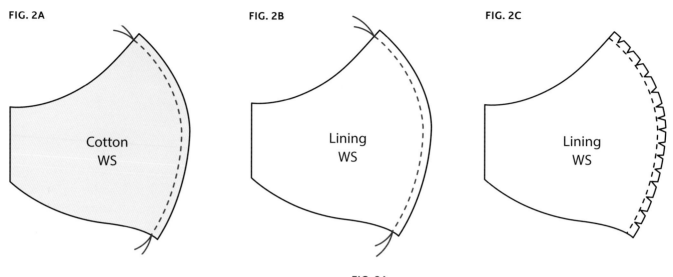

FIG. 2A

Cotton
WS

FIG. 2B

Lining
WS

FIG. 2C

Lining
WS

2. Place the outer mask pieces right sides together and stitch the front curved seam (fig. 2a). Repeat for the flannel mask pieces (fig. 2b). Along the curved edge, carefully clip perpendicular to the seam line in the seam allowance on both the outer mask and the flannel lining (fig. 2c). Press so that the seam allowance of the mask is to the left and the lining is to the right. Set aside the outer mask.

3. Fold the 3" (7.6cm) piece of bias tape in half, short ends aligned, and press to crease the center; unfold (fig. 3a). Position the bias tape approximately ½" (1.3cm) from the top edge, wrong side of tape to wrong side of lining, with the center crease of the tape aligned with the center seam of the lining. Pin. Stitch around three sides of the bias tape a few threads inside the edge, leaving one short end open (fig. 3b).

4. Insert the metal nosepiece into the casing, making sure it is completely inserted and that at least ⅛" (0.3cm) of the bias tape can be stitched down at the open end. If not, trim the nosepiece and re-insert. Stitch across the open end of the bias tape, securing the nosepiece in the casing (fig. 4). Remember, if you do not have a nosepiece, you can make a great substitute from an aluminum pie pan; see page 63.

FIG. 3A

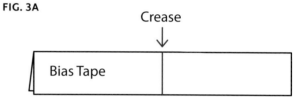

Crease

Bias Tape

FIG. 3B

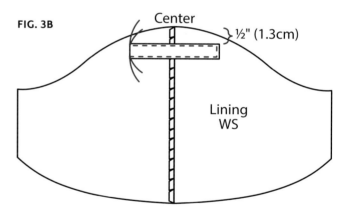

Center

½" (1.3cm)

Lining
WS

FIG. 4

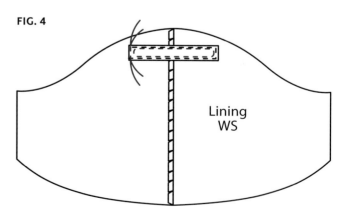

Lining
WS

FIG. 5

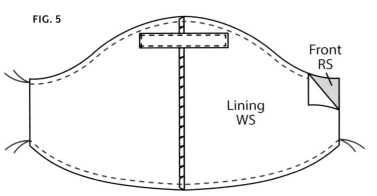

5. Place the outer mask and prepared lining right sides together and pin all the way around. Stitch across the bottom and the top with a ¼" (0.6cm) seam. Make sure to backstitch securely at the side edges (fig. 5).

FIG. 6A

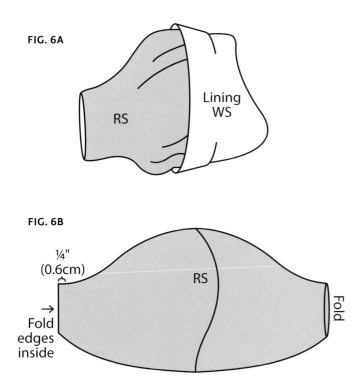

FIG. 6B

6. Turn the mask right side out through one of the open sides. This design takes a little tugging, as the opening is slightly small, but work slowly, pulling a little bit of fabric at a time. Once it is right side out, press firmly around the edges (fig. 6a). Fold the raw side edges to the inside ¼" (0.6cm) and press (fig. 6b).

FIG. 7

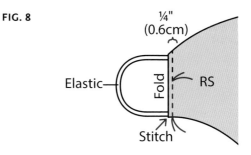

7. Insert one end of the elastic at the lower end of the side opening so that it overlaps ¼" (0.6cm) inside the mask. Pin. Insert the needle about 1" (2.5cm) above the elastic and stitch down to the end of the mask. Stitch back and forth several times at the lower edge to secure the elastic. Stop stitching and clip the threads (fig. 7).

FIG. 8

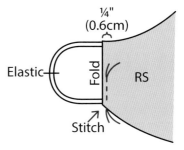

8. Turn the mask so that the top edge is now at the bottom. Insert the opposite end of the elastic. Pin, making sure your elastic isn't twisted. Insert the needle where you started stitching at the bottom of the mask and continue stitching to the top of the mask, stitching back and forth several times over the elastic to secure it. Repeat for the opposite side of the mask (fig. 8).

Tip

Metal nose bridge strips—for incorporating into face masks—can be purchased in bulk packages online if you plan to make multiple masks. If, however, you don't anticipate making many masks, an easy alternative is to cut a 2¾" x ¾" (7 x 1.9cm) rectangle from an aluminum pie pan, pizza pan, or other baking pan. Fold over ¼" (0.6cm) and ¼" (0.6cm) again lengthwise. Voilà! Instant nose bridge.

Window Pal Pillowcase

With reverse appliqué, you can create windows on this pillowcase to frame any little characters or motifs you choose. Pick superheroes, princesses, butterflies, dinosaurs, or anything that can bring a smile to the face of a little one.

MATERIALS

- 1¾ yard (1.6m) of fabric for pillowcase body, 42" (1.07m) wide
- ⅓ yard (31cm) of solid coordinating fabric for pillowcase band, 42" (1.07m) wide
- ¼ yard (23cm) of novelty print, 42" (1.07m) wide
- Circle template (page 67)
- Lightweight fusible interfacing
- 10" x 20" (25.4 x 50.8cm) strip of lightweight tear-away stabilizer
- ⅛ yard (11.4cm) lightweight iron-on interfacing
- Optional: Embroidery floss in three coordinating colors
- Optional: Embroidery hand sewing needle

TOOLS

- Universal sewing needle
- Sewing scissors
- Wash-away marker
- Fabric glue pen
- Seam gauge
- Clear ruler

CUTTING LIST

- From pillow body fabric:
  - 1 rectangle, 21½" x 52" (54.6 x 132cm), for pillow body
- From solid coordinating fabric:
  - 1 strip, 10" x 42" (25.4 x 106cm) long
- From novelty print:
  - 1 strip, 1⅝" x 42" (4.2 x 106cm) long
  - 3 motif squares, 4" (10.2cm), with a motif centered in each square
- From lightweight tear-away stabilizer:
  - 1 strip, 10" x 20" (25.4 x 50.8cm) long
- From lightweight interfacing:
  - 3 squares, 4" (10.2cm)

All seam allowances are ½" (1.3cm) unless otherwise noted.

Embellished Band

FIG. 1

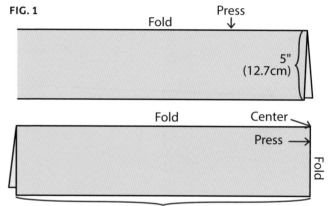

1. To find the centers of the pillow band, fold the solid strip in half lengthwise and press. Fold short end to short end and press. Open. You will be working on the lower right quadrant of your band to position the circles (fig. 1).

FIG. 2

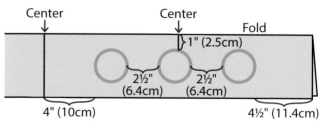

2. At the lengthwise center of the lower right quadrant, measure down 1" (2.5cm) and to the left ¼" (0.6cm). Center the 2½" (6.4cm) circle and trace. Trace one circle 2½" (6.4cm) to the right and left of the center traced circle (fig. 2).

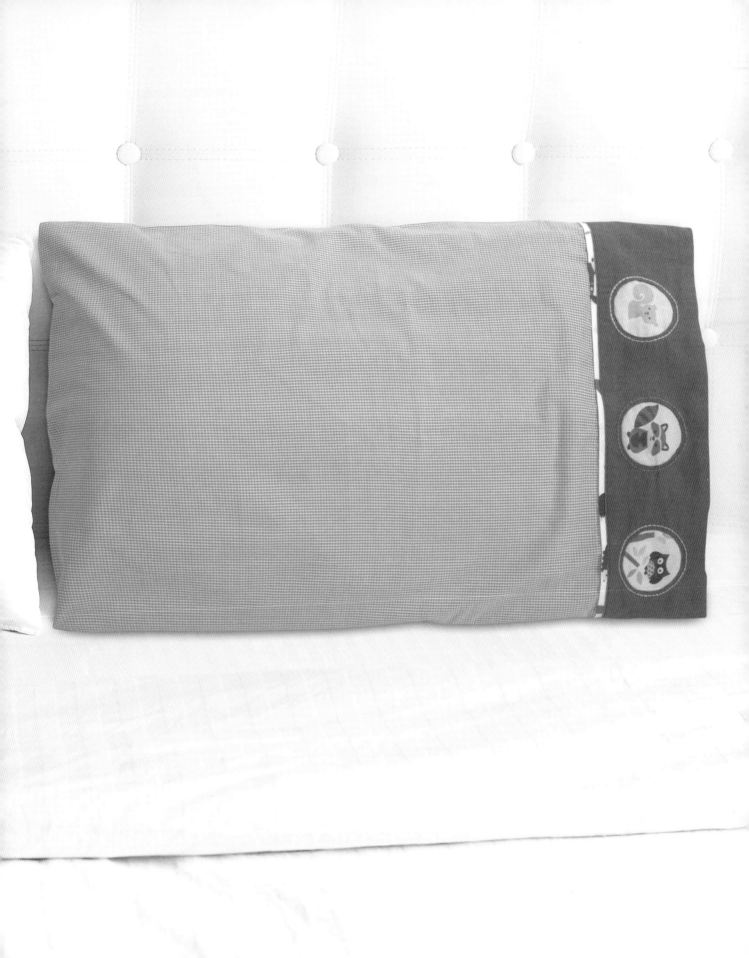

FIG. 3

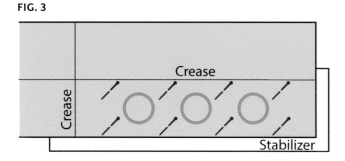

3. Unfold the band lengthwise and place a strip of tear-away stabilizer underneath your circle area. Pin to hold in place (fig. 3).

FIG. 4A

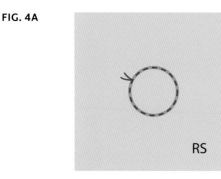

FIG. 4B

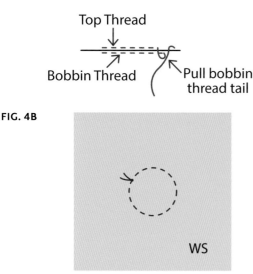

4. Thread the machine with a color to match the band fabric. Set it for straight stitching and use a clear foot (if available) and a stitch length of 2.0. Slowly stitch around the circle directly on the tracing line, pivoting as needed. If your machine has a needle down option, it is very helpful for stitching and pivoting curves (fig. 4a).

Do not use a fix function on your machine that secures your stitching to start and stop; you will want thread tails. Stitch to complete the circle. Stop and pull the project from the machine, clipping a thread tail at least 3" (7.6 cm) long. Pull the top thread to the back side and tie off (fig. 4b). Repeat for all three circles.

FIG. 5A

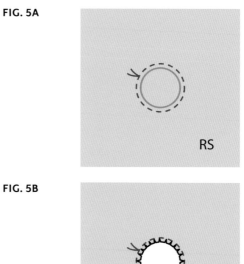

FIG. 5B

5. Using your wash-away marker, trace a second circle centered ¼" (0.6cm) inside the stitched circle (fig 5a). Cut out the inside of the circle on the traced line. Clip in every ¼" (0.6cm) of the seam allowance just up to the stitch line (fig. 5b).

FIG. 6

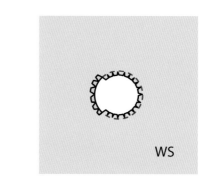

6. From the wrong side, lightly dot just outside the stitched circle with a fabric glue pen. Fold the seam allowance onto the back side, pressing it onto the adhesive with the tips of your fingers. The stitch line should be just at the edge of the open circle. Press with a steam iron on the setting that suits your fabric (fig. 6). Repeat for the remaining two circles.

7. Press iron-on interfacing to the back of each novelty square.

FIG. 7

RS

8. Position one of the three motifs underneath a circle opening so that it shows through as desired. Pin or glue to secure the right side of the square to the wrong side of the band. Repeat for the remaining motif squares and circle openings (fig. 7).

FIG. 8

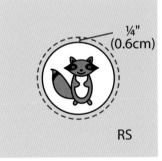

¼"
(0.6cm)

RS

9. Set the machine to a 2.5 stitch length and carefully stitch ¼" (0.6cm) around each circle opening. Work slowly, guiding your presser foot along the circle edge for a consistent width, and pivot when needed (fig. 8). Optional: If you are covering your stitching with a hand backstitch, you can use your machine's fix function or backstitch to secure your stitching. If you are leaving the machine stitch line visible, do not secure your stitching by machine. Once you've completed the circle, leave the thread tails, pull the top thread tail to the back side, and hand knot; refer to step 4.

FIG. 9A

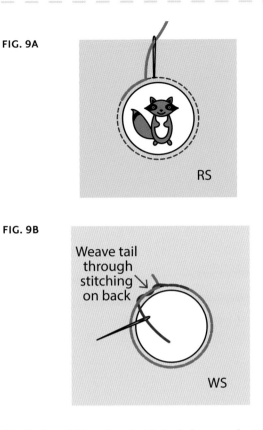

RS

FIG. 9B

Weave tail through stitching on back

WS

10. Optional: For a hand-stitched charm, select three coordinating embroidery floss colors and work hand backstitching directly over the machine stitching. To keep your stitches consistent, bring the needle up in the hole of one machine stitch, skip the next hole, and pierce down into the hole made by the second machine stitch (fig. 9a). Continue in this manner around the circle. Tie off on the back side when you've completed stitching around the circle and weave the tail through the stitching on the back side (fig. 9b).

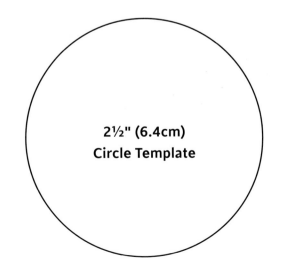

2½" (6.4cm)
Circle Template

FIG. 10

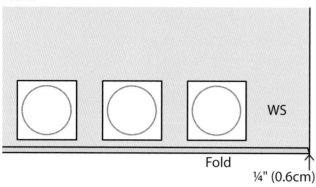

WS

Fold

¼" (0.6cm)

11. Fold the raw fabric edge below the circle embellishment ¼" (0.6cm) to the wrong side and press (fig. 10).

FIG. 11

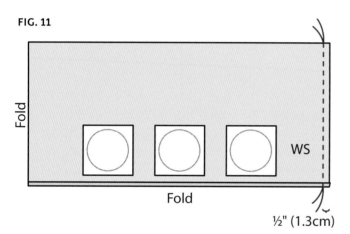

Fold

WS

Fold

½" (1.3cm)

12. Fold the wrong sides together to join the 9¾" (24.8cm) sides. Pin. Stitch with a ½" (2.5cm) seam allowance. Press the seam allowance open. Set the band aside (fig. 11).

Pillowcase Body

13. Fold 1⅝" x 42" (4.1 x 106.7cm) of novelty fabric in half lengthwise and press. Cut the strip into two 21" (53.3cm) pieces.

FIG. 12

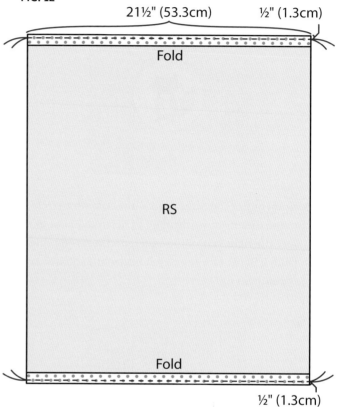

21½" (53.3cm)   ½" (1.3cm)

Fold

RS

Fold

½" (1.3cm)

14. On the top short edge of the pillowcase body (right side), place one trim piece, raw edges together. Stitch to join using a ½" (1.3cm) seam allowance. Repeat with the second trim strip on the lower short end of the pillowcase body (fig. 12).

FIG. 13

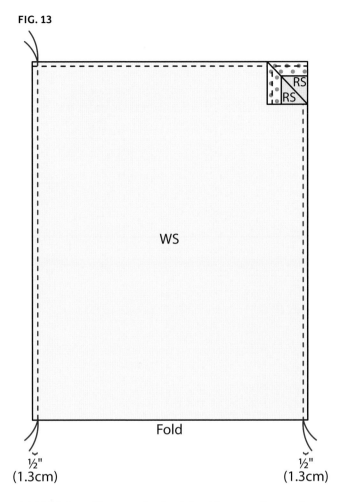

WS

Fold

½"
(1.3cm)

½"
(1.3cm)

15. Fold the pillowcase body right sides together and stitch the sides, making sure that the trim lines are aligned (fig. 13). Serge finish or trim to ¼" (0.6cm) and zigzag finish. Turn right side out and press.

Joining the Pillowcase Band

FIG. 14

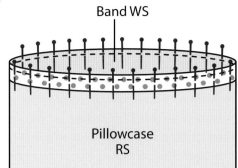

Band WS

Pillowcase RS

16. With the embellishment on the pillowcase band on the lower half, insert the band inside the pillowcase body, right side of band to wrong side of pillowcase. Align the band side seam to a pillowcase side seam with the raw edges of the pillowcase and band together. Pin (fig. 14).

17. Stitch the band to the pillowcase, sewing directly on top of the stitch line that joins the trim to the pillowcase. This will provide a consistent trim width on the outside of the pillowcase.

18. Press the seam allowance toward the band, and the trim toward the pillowcase. Flip the band to the right side and align the folded-under edge so that it just covers the seam line of the trim. Pin. Edge stitch the band in place (fig. 15).

FIG. 15

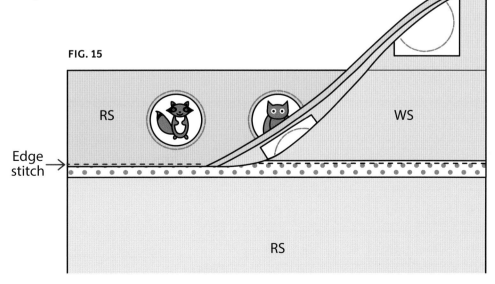

RS

WS

Edge stitch

RS

RS

Quilt-As-You-Go Lap Blanket

Keeping residents warm in care facilities is an ongoing battle, so it's never a mistake to have extra lap quilts on hand. This design couldn't be simpler for a first-time quilter to learn the basics. By using pre-cut charm packs, you don't have to worry about cutting out identical 5" (12.7cm) squares—that work is done for you—and the entire quilt can be made and finished on your home machine because it uses a quilt-as-you-go technique. This version, at 36½" x 32" (92.7 x 81.3cm), is smaller than a typical 50" to 60" (1.3 to 1.5m) lap quilt. The smaller size is lighter and fits more easily in wheelchairs. Plus, when you add the optional muff, it offers a soft and cozy place to keep hands warm.

MATERIALS

- 56 quilt squares, 5" (12.7cm), or two charm packs
- 1¼ yards (1.14m) of 48" (1.23m)–wide coordinating fabric for backing
- 40" x 44" (1.02 x 1.12m) rectangle of batting
- ¼ yard (23cm) of 48" (1.23m)–wide coordinating fabric for binding
- Optional: ⅓ yard (30cm) or fat quarter for muff
- Optional: ⅓ yard (30cm) fleece for muff

TOOLS

- Universal or quilting needle
- Rotary cutter
- Sewing scissors
- Thread to match
- Temporary spray adhesive

CUTTING LIST

- From coordinating binding fabric:
  - Multiple strips, 2¼" (5.7cm) wide, enough for 150" (3.81m) of binding
- From optional fabric and fleece:
  - 1 rectangle, 15" x 11½" (38.1 x 29.2cm)

FIG. 1

1a	2a	3a	4a	5a	6a	7a
1b	2b	3b	4b	5b	6b	7b
1c	2c	3c	4c	5c	6c	7c
1d	2d	3d	4d	5d	6d	7d
1e	2e	3e	4e	5e	6e	7e
1f	2f	3f	4f	5f	6f	7f
1g	2g	3g	4g	5g	6g	7g
1h	2h	3h	4h	5h	6h	7h

1. Lay out your charm squares in seven columns and eight rows in a pleasing colorway or pattern. Once you've laid out your squares, take a picture on your phone and check placement; a picture often reveals color masses and duplicate patterns missed with the naked eye. Once you've finalized your layout, mentally label the rows as A through H and the columns as 1 through 7. Flip the squares over and use a wash-away marker to write the identifier—1a, 1b, etc.—on each square. This will help prevent you from mixing up the squares when you sew them together (fig. 1).

The simple-to-add,
optional muff pocket is
lined with a soft fleece
and is an ideal way to
keep hands warm and
circulation flowing.

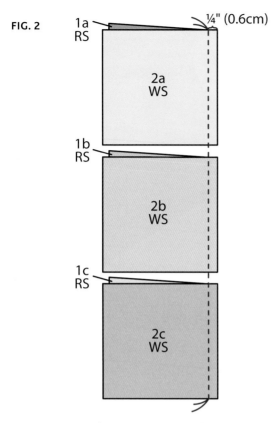

FIG. 2

1a RS

¼" (0.6cm)

2a WS

1b RS

2b WS

1c RS

2c WS

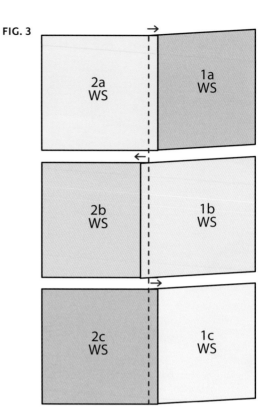

FIG. 3

2a WS | 1a WS

2b WS | 1b WS

2c WS | 1c WS

2. Place your column 1 squares with the column 2 squares on top, right sides together. Chain stitch with a ¼" (0.6cm) seam allowance (fig. 2), referring to Chain Stitching on page 21 if needed. Repeat by chaining your column 3 and 4 squares together with column 4 squares on top, and then your column 5 and 6 squares together with column 6 squares on top. Column 7 will stand alone for now. You should have three chains.

3. On each chain, press the pairs open, alternating the seam allowances for each pair in the opposite direction (fig. 3). Clip apart your chains and lay out your joined squares again in order.

4. Place your second chain pieces (column 3 and 4 squares) right sides together on top of your first chain pieces (column 1 and 2 squares) and pin each corresponding pair, nesting the seams. Chain stitch. Press open, again with the seam allowances for each in opposite directions (fig. 4).

5. Repeat step 4, adding your third chain pieces (column 5 and 6 squares). Press, then add the squares from column 7 to the right side of the column 6 squares. After pressing, cut the "chain" threads between the rows. You should now have eight rows of seven squares.

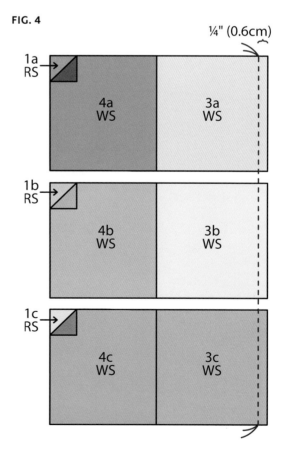

FIG. 4

¼" (0.6cm)

1a RS

4a WS | 3a WS

1b RS

4b WS | 3b WS

1c RS

4c WS | 3c WS

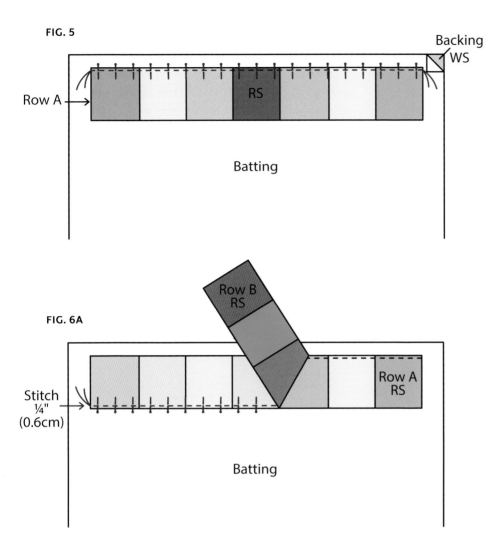

FIG. 5

Row A →

Backing WS

RS

Batting

FIG. 6A

Row B RS

Stitch ¼" (0.6cm) →

Row A RS

Batting

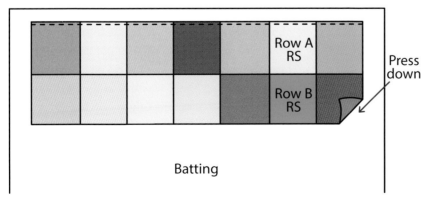

FIG. 6B

Row A RS

Row B RS

Press down

Batting

6. For home sewing and a quick finish, use the quilt-as-you-go method. You will be joining the rows and quilting at the same time. Place your backing right side down on a flat surface and center your batting on top, aligning the top edge. Now take your first row and place it wrong side down 1" to 1½" (2.5 to 3.8cm) from the top of the batting/backing, making sure it is straight across. Pin generously through all layers, making sure the backing is smooth (fig. 5).

7. Make sure your threads are a color that is flattering to the backing, as it will show as topstitching on the back of your finished quilt. Stitch across the top with a ¼" (0.6cm) seam allowance. Remove from the machine and smooth out all layers on a flat surface. To help keep each row secure and flat against the batting as you stitch on the next row, you can lightly spray that section of batting underneath with a mist of temporary spray adhesive before pressing down.

8. Place your second row right side down directly on top of the first row so that the top edge of the second row is aligned with the bottom edge of the first row (the second row should be upside down). Nest the seams between each square and place a pin on each side of the nested seams through all layers to make sure they stay aligned while sewing. Check to make sure the backing is smooth. Stitch through all the layers with a ¼" (0.6cm) seam allowance (fig. 6a). Press this second row down, wrong sides against the batting (fig. 6b).

FIG. 7

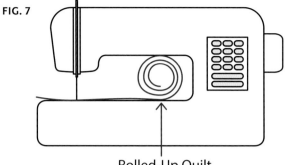

Rolled-Up Quilt

9. Join the remaining rows in order, using a ¼" (0.6cm) seam allowance and making sure the seams are nested and the backing and batting are smooth. Once you join the fourth row, you will want to turn and quilt from the other side so that you never have more than half of the quilt in the throat of your machine. Whenever you have extra quilted fabric in the throat of your machine, roll it up so it moves more easily as you stitch (fig. 7).

FIG. 8

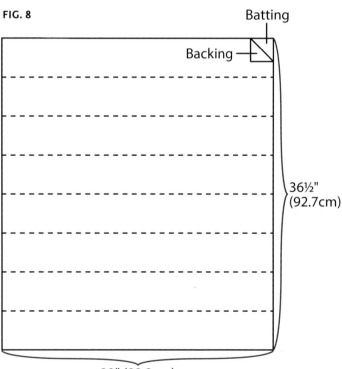

Batting

Backing

36½"
(92.7cm)

32" (82.3cm)

10. Once you've joined the final row, press flat and stitch down the bottom edge through all layers using a ¼" (0.6cm) seam allowance. Trim off the excess batting and backing even with the quilt top. Your finished quilt should measure approximately 36½" long x 32" wide (92.7 x 82.3cm) with neat horizontal quilting stitches visible on the backing (fig. 8).

11. Finish your quilt with a ¼" (0.6cm) binding, referring to Binding Quilt Edges on page 23.

Optional Muff

The muff will be applied over six blocks, starting on the second row, block three, and ending on the third row, block five.

FIG. 9

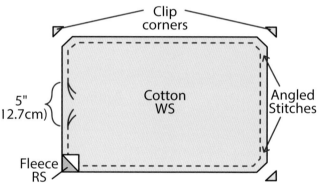

Clip corners

5"
12.7cm)

Cotton
WS

Angled
Stitches

Fleece
RS

1. Place the fleece and outer fabric rectangles right sides together, pin the edges, and stitch with a ½" (1.3cm) seam allowance all around, making one to two angled stitches at each corner to create sharper points when turned. Leave a 5" (12.7cm) opening between the beginning and end of the stitch line. Backstitch at the beginning and end of the stitching to secure. Clip across the corners (fig. 9).

2. Turn the muff right side out through the opening. Press, turn under the opening in line with the muff edge, pin or glue, and topstitch down the short sides with a ¼" (0.6cm) seam allowance.

FIG. 10

Stitch
across

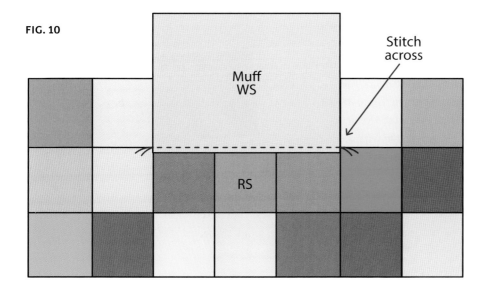

3. Position the muff right side down on the quilt, centered and overlapping the join between the first and second rows by an even ½" (1.3cm). Pin generously. Straight stitch with a ½" (1.3cm) seam allowance through all layers. The goal is to position your stitching so that it is in line with the quilting line on the back (fig. 10). Backstitch several times at the beginning and end of your stitching.

FIG. 11

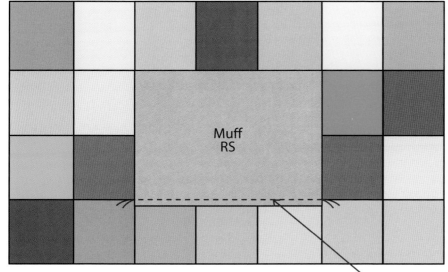

Stitch across

4. Fold the muff down so that the fleece lining is against the quilt. The lower edge of the muff should extend approximately ¼" (0.6cm) past the join between the third and fourth rows. Topstitch with a ¼" (0.6cm) seam allowance, backstitching to secure your stitching at the beginning and end of the stitching (fig. 11).

Memory-Care Fidget Mat

This is a fun way to help engage the minds of memory-care patients who are struggling with everyday tasks. It's also an ideal project for practicing your sewing and quilting skills, from edge stitching and making buttonholes to binding and hand sewing buttons. While instructions and supplies are for the fidget mat shown, there are all sorts of notions and ideas you can add to your own mat. I've seen them with belts to buckle, yarn to braid, a change purse with a clasp opening, a fabric glasses case—you name it. If it can be stitched, you'll find it on a fidget mat.

MATERIALS

- Memory-Care Fidget Mat pattern piece: Pocket
- ⅓ yard (30cm) of each of five different-colored fleeces
- 1¼ yard (1.14m) of medium-weight fusible interfacing
- Scraps of coordinating cotton for tabs, pocket, and placket
- ¼ yard (22.9cm) of coordinating cotton for binding
- Parachute buckle for 1" (2.5cm) strap
- Large hook and D-ring for 1" (2.5cm) strap
- 14" (35.6cm) of 1" (2.5cm)–wide parachute strap in two different colors
- ¾ yard (69cm) of spaghetti bias, ribbon, or narrow cording
- 18" (45.7cm) of ¹⁄₁₆" (1.6mm)–wide cord elastic
- 10 to 12 beads (make sure holes are large enough to thread through doubled elastic cord)
- Zipper with ring pull
- 48" (1.23m) shoelace
- 5 buttons with ⅞" (2.2cm) shank
- 4 two- or four-hole buttons, ½" (1.3cm)
- 12" (30.5cm) of eyelet belting trim
- 6" (15.2cm) of ⅝" (1.6cm) grosgrain ribbon
- 15" (38.1cm) of double-fold bias tape, ½" (1.3cm) if purchased or ⅜" (1cm) if self-made
- Lace doily or hankie

TOOLS

- Tube turner
- Rotary cutter
- Sewing scissors
- Seam gauge
- 10½" (26.7cm) square ruler
- Clear ruler
- Large-eye needle
- Hand sewing needle
- White thread and other thread colors to match straps and ribbon
- Machine edge foot
- Machine buttonhole foot/attachment
- Tear-away stabilizer
- Fabric glue pen
- Wash-away marker
- Glass head pins
- Seam ripper

CUTTING LIST

- From each of three fleece colors:
  - 1 rectangle, 12" x 24" (30.5 x 61cm), for backing
- From interfacing:
  - 4 squares, 9½" (24.1cm)
  - 1 rectangle, 9½" x 19" (24.1 x 48.3cm)
- From cotton:
  - 4 strips, 2" x 30" (5.1 x 76.2cm) long, for binding

Preparing the Sections

1. Using a 10½" (26.7cm) square ruler or clear ruler, trace four 10½" (26.7cm) blocks, each on a different color fleece. Leaving at least ½" (1.3cm) beyond the traced line on all four sides, cut around each traced block. Repeat for the fifth fleece color, tracing a 10½" x 20" (26.7 x 50.8cm) rectangle and leaving a 1½" (3.8cm) edge around the tracing (fig. 1).

FIG. 1

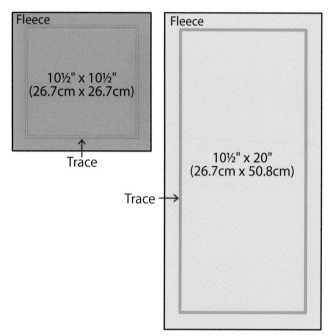

2. Following the manufacturer's instructions, center and fuse the interfacing squares to the four fleece squares. Repeat for the fleece rectangle. Tip: To help avoid crushing the pile of your fleece, place a bath towel on the surface of your ironing board and then place each piece face down on the towel before pressing the interfacing to the wrong side.

3. Working one block at a time, begin to add your fidget accessories to each block, making sure you keep any tabs or applications at least 1" (2.5cm) inside your traced blocks, with the exception of the faux bias tape neckline (rectangle block) and the spaghetti bias tie (buttons block).

Making Tabs for the Bead Band, Shoestring Eyelets, Zipper Pull, and Shirt Placket End

For many fidget accessories, all that is needed is to pin the element on the square in the desired position (refer to the mat diagram for placement) and cover the raw ends in a fabric tab.

FIG. 2

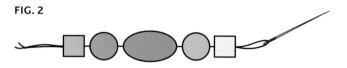

1. For this mat, start by preparing the following:
- Cut the zipper to 8¼" (21cm) long.
- Cut two shoestring eyelet pieces to 5½" (14cm) long and position them approximately ¼" (0.6cm) apart.
- Thread a large-eye needle with 20" (51.2cm) of elastic cord so the cord is doubled. Thread the needle and cord through the beads so that you have an approximately 6" (15.2cm) section of beads centered on 10" (25.4cm) of doubled elastic. Cut the elastic to remove the needle and tie the elastic together on both ends with a small knot (fig. 2).

FIG. 3

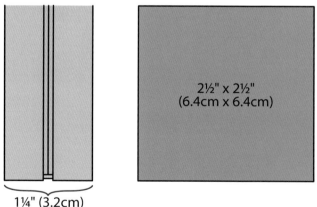

2. Measure horizontally across the end of the element being applied. For example, the end of the zipper pull on the mat shown measures 1¼" (3.2cm) across. Cut a 2½" (6.4cm) cotton strip that is two times this width ([1¼" + 1¼" = 2½"] [3.2 + 3.2cm = 6.4cm]) and 2½" (6.4cm) long. For this example, that is 2½" (6.4cm) square (fig. 3).

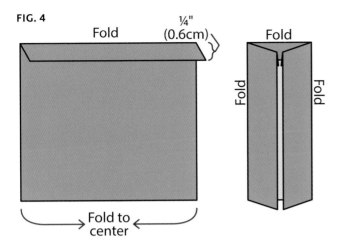

FIG. 4

Fold

¼"
(0.6cm)

Fold

Fold   Fold

Fold to
center

3. Fold one 2½" (6.4cm) end to the wrong side ¼" (0.6cm) and press. Fold each long edge to the wrong side so the raw edges meet in the center and press (fig. 4).

FIG. 5

½"
(1.3cm)

Fold

Fold

Fold

4. Insert the lower edge of your zipper (or other trim) into the (unfolded) short end of the tab with the wrong side facing up. At least ½" (1.3cm) of the trim/zipper end should be encased inside the tab (fig. 5).

FIG. 6

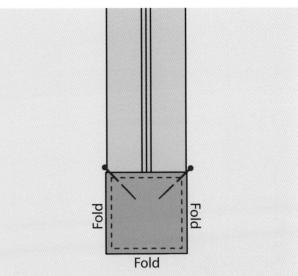

Fold

Fold

Fold

5. Fold the tab on itself, wrong sides together, so the folded-under edge is flush with the raw edge. Pin and carefully stitch all four sides of the tab through all layers with a scant ⅛" (0.3cm) seam allowance. Pivot at each corner and secure the stitch line with a backstitch where it meets (fig. 6).

6. Follow this sequence of steps to assemble the bead band on its own block as well as the shoestring eyelets and zipper pull on the rectangle block. The shirt placket end will be covered later, under Shirt Placket Block.

Ribbon-Trimmed Pocket Block

Fill a sweet little pocket with a lace doily or a vintage hankie. Just make sure to tether your inserted item with a length of knotted thread tailing so it can be removed easily but won't get lost.

1. Cut out the pocket from cotton fabric using the pocket pattern. Using wash-away marker, mark the ribbon placement line. Cut out half a pocket from fusible interfacing using the pattern fold line as a guide.

FIG. 7

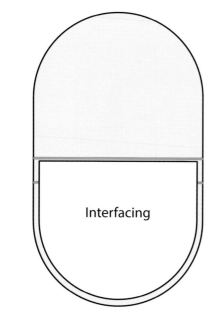

Interfacing

2. Following the manufacturer's instructions, adhere the interfacing to the wrong side of the pocket front (fig. 7).

FIG. 8

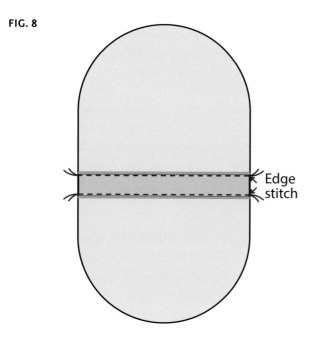

Edge stitch

3. Align the top edge of a strip of ¾" (1.9cm)–wide grosgrain ribbon with the placement line. Pin or use a fabric glue pen to secure in place. Edge stitch just inside the long edges of the ribbon on both sides to attach. If your machine has a guide foot, this is a perfect opportunity to use it. Simply snap on the foot and move your needle a few positions to the left (fig. 8).

FIG. 9

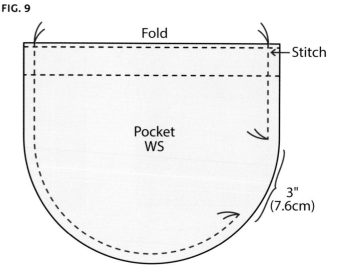

Fold

Stitch

Pocket
WS

3"
(7.6cm)

4. Fold the pocket in half wrong sides together, matching the edges, and pin. Stitch around the pocket with a ¼" (0.6cm) allowance, leaving a 3" (7.6cm) opening in one side and securing the stitch line at the beginning and end (fig. 9).

FIG. 10

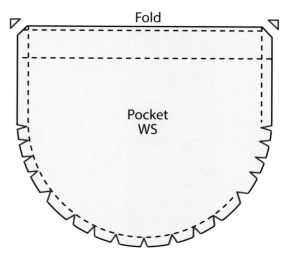

Fold

Pocket
WS

5. Clip around the curves just to the stitch lines. Clip across the corners. Turn the pocket right side out through the opening. Turn under the raw edges of the opening in line with the finished pocket edges and press (fig. 10).

FIG. 11

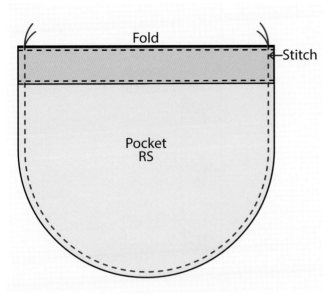

6. Position your pocket on the corresponding block. Pin and stitch around with a ⅛" (0.3cm) seam allowance, securing with a backstitch or fix stitch at the beginning and end of your stitch line (fig. 11).

FIG. 12

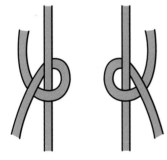

7. Create a knotted thread tether for your hankie/doily. Separate a 12" to 15" (30.5 to 38.1cm) piece of embroidery floss into two sections of three threads each. Thread a crewel needle with one three-strand section. Knot the end and make a few stitches to secure to the corner of your hankie/doily. Repeat, securing the second three-strand section to the same place on your hankie/doily. Place your hankie/doily on a flat surface and tape it down or weigh it down with a book so it won't move while you knot. You will be knotting with one three-strand section over the other three-strand section. Make a simple knot looping to the right, then make a second knot with a loop to the left. Repeat, knotting from left to right, until you have a knotted strand that is at least 3" (7.6cm) long (fig. 12).

FIG. 13

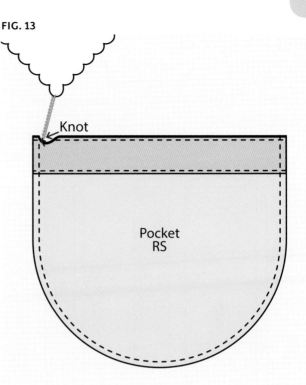

8. Re-thread all six strands of floss through the needle and tack the end of the tether to the wrong side of the pocket next to a side seam line. Knot and clip the thread tail (fig. 13).

Shirt Placket Block

This faux placket allows aging fingers to work on their dexterity and also lets you practice using your machine buttonhole and button functions as well as work with bias curves.

FIG. 14

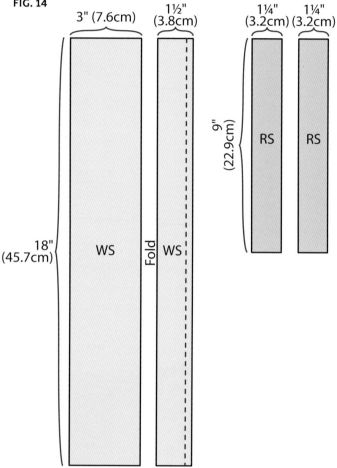

FIG. 15

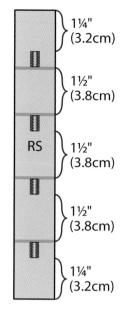

2. On one piece, mark your buttonhole positioning. Machine buttonholes generally stitch out from front to back, so mark the starting point for the first buttonhole 1¼" (3.2cm) from the top edge, and stitch the succeeding buttonholes 1½" (3.8cm) apart. This assumes a ½" (1.3cm) button (fig. 15).

FIG. 16

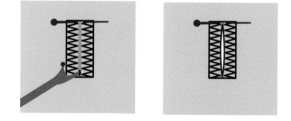

1. Cut a strip of fabric 3" x 18" (7.6 x 45.7cm) long. Fold right sides together, matching raw long edges. Press. Stitch the length of the raw edge with a ¼" (0.6cm) seam allowance to create a tube. Turn the tube right side out. Press with the seam to one side, then cut into two 9" (22.9cm) pieces. A tube turner is a helpful tool to use here (fig. 14).

3. Once all buttonholes are stitched, open each by placing a straight pin horizontally across the top thread of each buttonhole. Insert a seam ripper just inside the bottommost thread and carefully run it up the center of the buttonhole, ending at the pin. The pin will keep the seam ripper from cutting though the threads at the top of the buttonhole (fig. 16).

FIG. 17

4. Stitch down each side of the buttonhole placket strip ¼" (0.6cm) from the edges (fig. 17).

FIG. 18

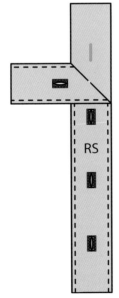

5. Place the buttonhole strip directly on top of the remaining placket strip and use a wash-away marker to mark the button placement through the opening of each buttonhole (fig. 18).

6. Stitch on the buttons by hand or by machine, making sure they are not too tightly stitched to the surface. Make sure to drop your feed dogs before using your machine to apply a button.

FIG. 19A

Fold   Fold

¼"
(0.6cm)

FIG. 19B

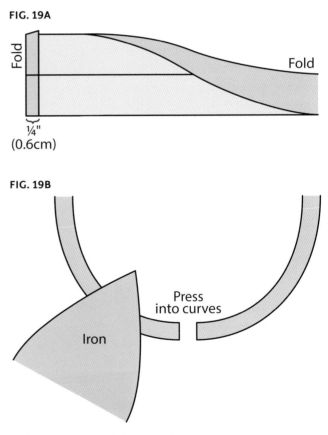

Press
into curves

Iron

7. Cut two pieces of double-fold bias tape 6½" (16.5cm) long. Open up the tape and turn under ¼" (0.6cm) on one short end of each piece. Press (fig. 19a). Refold the sides into place and press the bias tape into a curve; refer to the photograph (fig. 19b).

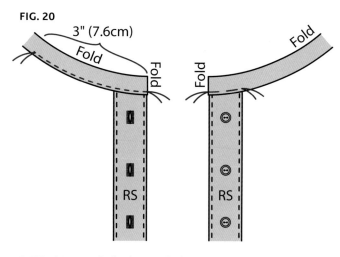

FIG. 20

3" (7.6cm)

Fold · Fold · Fold · Fold · Fold

RS · RS

8. Working with the buttonhole strip, insert the top raw end inside the turned-back folded end of the bias tape up to the crease. The back half of the bias tape should be folded to the back side and the lower edges aligned. Edge stitch the seam allowances, stitching along the lower edge of the bias tape through all layers, securing the strip. Continue stitching together the bias tape for approximately 3" (7.6cm) beyond the buttonhole strip edge. Set aside. Repeat with the button strip, but just baste stitch and do not continue stitching on the bias tape beyond the strip edge (fig. 20).

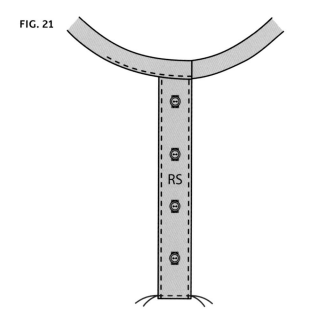

FIG. 21

RS

9. Button the strips together to make sure the bias edges align. Stitch the strips together across the bottom edge using a ¼" (0.6cm) seam allowance (fig. 21).

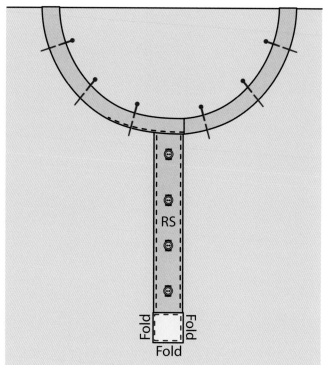

FIG. 22

RS

Fold · Fold · Fold

10. Position the placket with bias tape attached on the center section of the mat where desired and apply a tab to secure it in place at the bottom edge (fig. 22). Refer to page 78 for tab instructions.

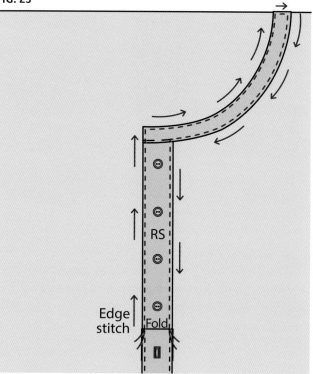

FIG. 23

RS

Edge stitch · Fold

11. Unbutton the placket and fold the top section down. Pin the button strip to the mat, curving the neckline bias up so that the end extends beyond the top traced line of your block. Beginning where the buttonhole strip is folded back, stitch a scant ⅛" (0.3cm) up one side of the button placket and around the bias neck curve. Then stitch the other side of the bias neck curve and down the opposite side of the placket until you reach the point where the buttonhole strip is folded back. Backstitch your stitching to secure when you start and stop. This button half of the placket should be securely stitched to the mat (fig. 23).

FIG. 24

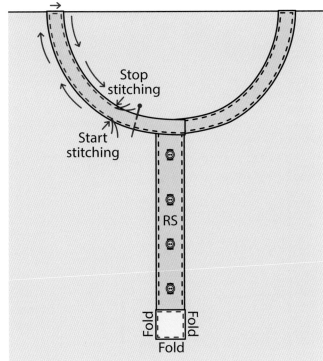

12. The buttonhole strip is not stitched down to the mat. Button it and curve the bias neckband to mirror-image the neckband on the opposite side, making sure the end extends beyond the traced line of your block. Stitch down both sides of the bias tape, starting where your stitch line ended when you applied the bias to the button strip, so approximately 2" (5.1cm) beyond the placket (fig. 24).

13. Hand stitch a snap to the corner of the neckband bias, adding another fastener element.

Buckles Block

There are all sorts of buckles, hooks, and fasteners on the notions wall of your local sewing store. Pick the ones that appeal to you. The two styles here accommodate a 1½" (3.8cm) parachute strap, which is easy to apply.

FIG. 25

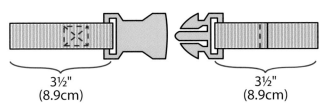

1. Directions for securing the cord to the fastener are included in the packaging. Essentially, weave the strip through the bar, fold under the raw edge, and straight stitch to secure (fig. 25). You will want at least a 3½" (8.9cm) length of strap once attached.

2. Once you've applied your strap to the fastener buckle, snap them together. Position them on your mat, folding under the raw end of the strap on each end approximately 1" (2.5cm), and pin. Make sure there is a slight give in the straps so they're not too tight and difficult to fasten and unfasten.

FIG. 26

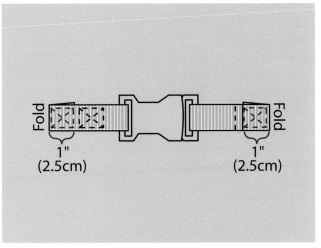

3. Using a thread color to match, and stitching through the folded-under strap end, stitch a 1" (2.5cm) square, pivoting at each corner, then stitch an X from corner to corner. Repeat for the end of each strap (fig. 26).

Buttons Block

For this square, you can machine-apply buttons with two or four holes, or you can practice stitching on shank buttons by hand. If you don't have any spaghetti bias, which is sold by the yard, a ¼" (0.6cm)–wide grosgrain ribbon or cording will suffice.

FIG. 27

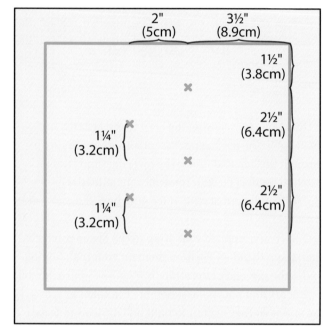

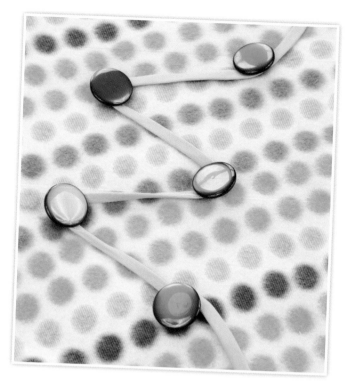

1. Using a wash-away marker, mark the positioning for three buttons down one side of your square, approximately 1½" (3.8cm) from the top, 2½" (6.4cm) apart, and 3½" (8.9cm) from the side of your traced block. Mark the positioning for two buttons approximately 2" (5.1cm) to the left and offset between the column of three buttons (fig. 27).

2. Hand stitch or apply the buttons by machine. If you are using two-hole or four-hole buttons, stitch with a buffer underneath the button so there is some room to wrap ribbon between the mat and the button.

FIG. 28

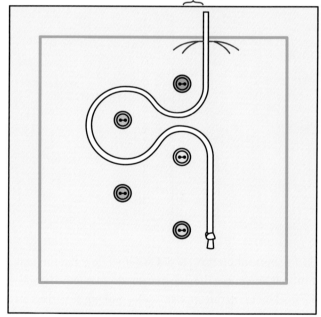

3. Cut an 18" (45.7cm) strip of spaghetti bias and pin it to the top of the traced block line, approximately ½" (1.3cm) to the right of the topmost button. Baste just inside the traced block line (fig. 28). Tie the spaghetti bias in a knot at the end.

Finishing

1. Using a clear quilting ruler, check that the traced block lines are the same size as originally traced. If not, retrace, centering the elements, and cut out each block on the traced lines.

FIG. 29

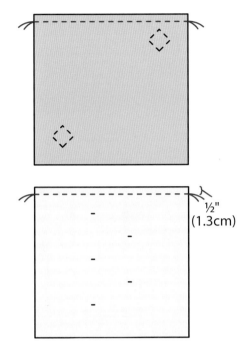

2. With right sides together, stitch the lower edge of the buckle block to the top edge of the bead band block with a ½" (1.3cm) seam allowance. Repeat, stitching the bottom of the buttons block to the top of the ribbon-trimmed pocket block. Press open the seams with a warm iron (fig. 29).

FIG. 30

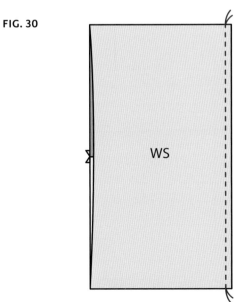

3. Stitch the joined blocks to the sides of the center rectangle block, one section at a time, using a ½" (1.3cm) seam allowance. Press the seams open with a warm iron. Joined, the mat top should measure approximately 20" x 29½" (50.8 x 75cm) (fig. 30).

FIG. 31

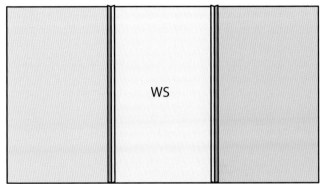

4. Stitch together your three backing rectangles along the 24" (61cm) edges. Press open the seams with a warm iron (fig. 31).

FIG. 32

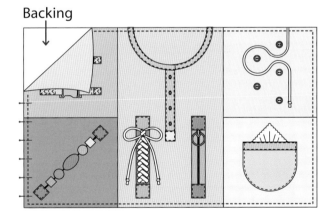

5. Center your mat top on your backing, wrong sides together, and cut away the excess backing fabric so the mat and backing are the same size. Pin around all four edges generously. Baste around the edges with a ½" (1.3cm) seam allowance (fig. 32).

6. Join the binding strips and bind the quilt with a ½" (2.5cm) binding. Refer to Joining Binding Ends on page 22 and Binding Quilt Edges on page 23. Weave the shoestring through the eyelets.

Arm Sling Cast Cover

I hope you never have to sew this for anyone but a teddy bear. However, if you have a friend or child in need, use this as an opportunity to bring them cheer with a bright and colorful fabric that reflects their personal style. If you need larger or smaller than the patterns in this book, simply measure from the back of your elbow to the middle of your pinky and add 1" (2.5cm) for a seam allowance.

MATERIALS

- Arm Sling Cast Cover pattern pieces: A, B, C, D (in desired size)
- Two fat quarters of cotton quilting fabric, 18" x 22" (45.7 x 55.9cm)
- 40" (1.02m) of 1" (2.5cm) webbing, 32" (81cm) for shoulder strap
- 8" (20.3cm) of 1" (2.5cm) webbing, 32" (81cm) for shoulder strap for front strap
- 8" x 5" (20.3 x 12.7cm) rectangle of craft felt or batting for neck pad
- 10" x 5" (25.4 x 12.7cm) piece of cotton fabric for neck pad (you will only need extra fabric for this if cutting out the large sling; for all other sizes, there is enough left on the fat quarter for the neck pad)
- 1" (2.5cm) side release buckle

MATERIALS FOR BEAR SLING

- Arm Sling Cast Cover pattern piece: Teddy Bear
- Two pieces of cotton quilting fabric, 8" x 7" (20.3 x 17.8cm)
- 23" (58.4cm) of 1" (2.5cm) webbing or ribbon
- 1" (2.5cm) side release buckle
- Note: Use a ½" (1.3cm) seam allowance for bear sling

TOOLS

- Sewing scissors
- Small safety pin
- Glass head pins
- Seam ripper
- Thread to match
- Seam gauge
- Wash-away marker
- Tube turner
- Optional: rubber band, hair tie, or clip for keeping webbing out of the way during assembly

FINISHED SLING SIZES

- Large/Adult: 16.5" x 7.5" (41.9 x 19.1cm)
- Medium: 15" x 6.75" (38.1 x 17.1cm)
- Small: 13" x 6.75" (33 x 17.1cm)
- Bear/Doll: 5" x 3.5" (12.7 x 8.9cm)

FIG. 1

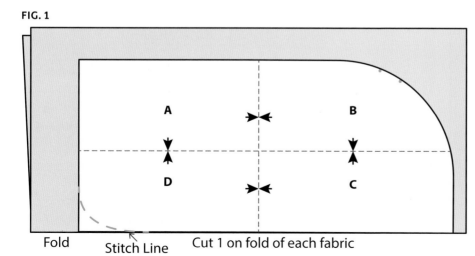

Fold   Stitch Line   Cut 1 on fold of each fabric

1. Trace the sling pattern pieces for your desired size, making sure to include all markings. Tape the pattern together as instructed, then pin the pattern onto your two folded fat quarters as shown (fig. 1). Cut it out.

Tip

Matching kids' and stuffed animals' slings can be a great comfort item to children.

FIG. 2A

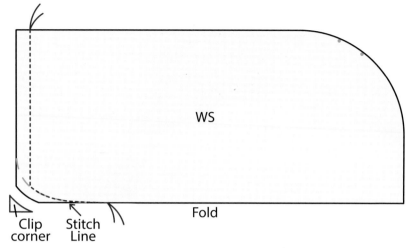

Clip corner Stitch Line Fold

WS

FIG. 2B

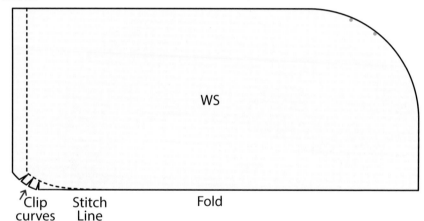

Clip curves Stitch Line Fold

WS

FIG. 3

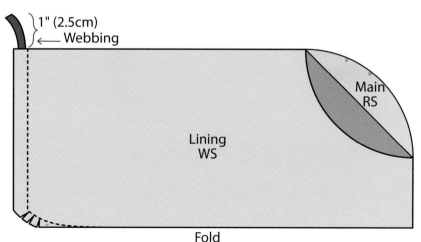

1" (2.5cm)
Webbing

Main RS

Lining WS

Fold

2. Turn the main fabric inside out and, using a ½" (1.3cm) seam allowance, stitch down the straight back edge, following the dashed curve line and ending at the bottom fold. Clip off the corner bottom edge, leaving a ½" (1.3cm) seam allowance around the curve (fig. 2a). Clip the curves, then press the seam allowance to the left (fig. 2b). Repeat with the lining fabric, but this time, when pressing, iron your seam allowance to the right to reduce the bulk you will have when it is time to sew the layers together.

3. Turn the main fabric right side out, leaving the lining fabric inside out. Center your long shoulder strap webbing to the back seam, in between the two sling layers, leaving 1" (2.5cm) of it sticking out of the top, and pin (fig. 3). Note: Here is where the clip, rubber band, or hair tie comes in handy. I roll up my excess webbing and clip it or wrap an elastic band around it to keep it out of the way while I'm sewing my layers together.

FIG. 4A

Female End of Side Release Buckle

8" (20.3cm) Webbing

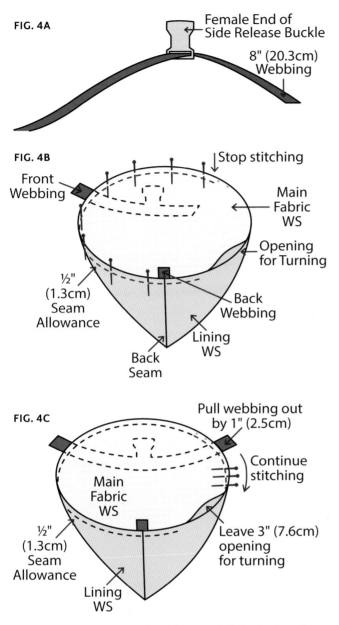

FIG. 4B

Stop stitching

Front Webbing

Main Fabric WS

Opening for Turning

½" (1.3cm) Seam Allowance

Back Webbing

Back Seam

Lining WS

FIG. 4C

Pull webbing out by 1" (2.5cm)

Continue stitching

Main Fabric WS

½" (1.3cm) Seam Allowance

Leave 3" (7.6cm) opening for turning

Lining WS

4. Take the short piece of webbing and slide the female end of the side release buckle onto the strap. The closed, back end of the buckle will be down toward your lining fabric, while the open end will be up toward your main fabric (fig. 4a). Pin one end of short webbing at the marks you made on the front of the sling, in between the main fabric and the lining on the left side of the sling, and leave 1" (2.5cm) of webbing sticking out. Pin the layers. Using a ½" (1.3cm) seam allowance, stitch the layers together, starting just to the right of the center back of the sling, continuing to 1" (2.5cm) from the webbing-placement marks on the right side of the sling, and backstitch a bit to secure (fig. 4b). Take out all the pins you have placed

so far, reach in between the layers, and pull out the free end of the short webbing. Pin the end in between the placement marks, making sure the strap is not twisted. Leave 1" (2.5cm) sticking out above the layers as before. Continue stitching layers around the sling, leaving a 3" (7.6cm) opening for turning (fig. 4c). Turn right side out.

FIG. 5A

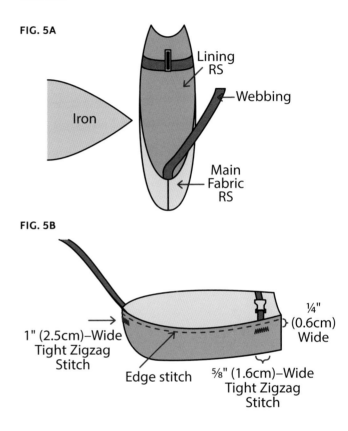

Lining RS

Webbing

Iron

Main Fabric RS

FIG. 5B

1" (2.5cm)–Wide Tight Zigzag Stitch

Edge stitch

¼" (0.6cm) Wide

⅝" (1.6cm)–Wide Tight Zigzag Stitch

5. Arrange the lining down into the main fabric layer and press the sling and all sewn edges. Be particularly careful when ironing over areas with webbing if you used nylon webbing instead of cotton—otherwise you may melt it (fig. 5a). Edge stitch the opening closed and continue edge stitching around the top of the sling. Drop down ¼" (0.6cm) below your edge stitch and, using a very tight zigzag stitch, sew a ⅝" (1.6cm)–long reinforcing line over the webbing inside the sling on each front side to keep it from pulling out under pressure. Repeat for the webbing on the back of the sling but stitch a 1" (2.5cm) line across it (fig. 5b). Optional: You can use a satin stitch for reinforcing the stitch instead of a tight zigzag. (A satin stitch is a zigzag stitch with a narrower length.)

FIG. 6A

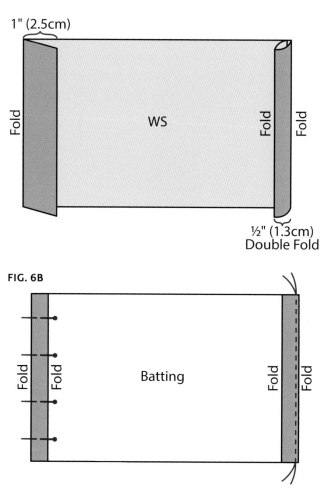

1" (2.5cm)

Fold

Fold

Fold

WS

½" (1.3cm)
Double Fold

FIG. 6B

Fold

Fold

Batting

Fold

Fold

FIG. 7A

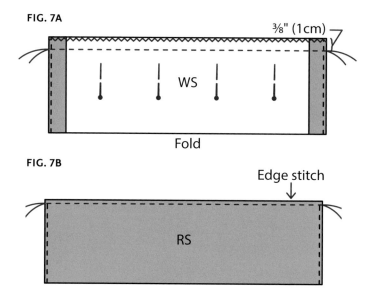

⅜" (1cm)

WS

Fold

FIG. 7B

Edge stitch

RS

7. Fold the neck pad in half lengthwise and, with right sides and raw edges together, secure with pins. Using a ⅜" (1cm) seam allowance, stitch together. Serge or zigzag the raw edges to keep them from fraying. Clip loose threads and turn right side out (fig. 7a). Press your neck pad so that the seam you made is to the side, then edge stitch only along the side with the seam (fig. 7b).

6. Take the rectangle of 10" x 5" (25.4 x 12.7cm) cotton fabric for the neck pad, fold each short end over by 1" (2.5cm) toward the wrong side, and press. Lift up the fold and press the raw edge down by ½" (1.3cm) toward the crease, fold over, and press again. You will end up with a ½" (1.3cm) double fold on each end (fig. 6a). Lay the 8" x 5" (20.3 x 12.7cm) piece of batting/padding on top of the wrong side of the fabric, with the short ends just under each folded edge of the fabric, and pin. Edge stitch each fold, being sure to catch the padding under the stitches (fig. 6b).

FIG. 8

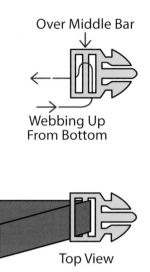

Over Middle Bar

Webbing Up From Bottom

Top View

Bottom View

9. Once your webbing is threaded through the buckle, adjust the sling to fit. Double-fold the raw edge of the webbing by folding it over by ½" (1.3cm) twice, then stitch it down securely (fig. 9). At this point, if you see that you are going to have way too much strap left hanging after adjusting, you can trim a bit off before you stitch the webbing.

10. Slide your completed neck pad over the shoulder strap webbing. You are ready to go! The neck pad is also the perfect way to hide your excess strap.

8. Take the male end of your side release buckle and feed the shoulder strap webbing up from under the front of buckle, over the middle center bar of the buckle, and down through the back of the buckle. When threaded correctly, the webbing is locked in place when the buckle is lying flat and is fully adjustable when the buckle is at an angle (fig. 8).

FIG. 9

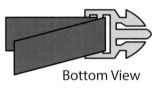

Top stitch

Fold

Webbing

Fold

½" (1.3cm) Double Fold

Fat Quarter Wheelchair/ Walker Caddy

Five coordinating fat quarters (two for lining, two for outer fabric and pockets, and one for binding) make it easy to select fabrics for this handy caddy that straps to a walker or wheelchair to keep tissues, books, glasses, and more in a pretty place with easy access.

MATERIALS

- 5 coordinating fat quarters of quilting cotton fabric, 18" x 22" (45.7 x 55.9cm)
- 1 zipper, at least 13" (33.cm) long
- 2 yards (1.83m) of 1" (2.5cm)–wide webbing for strap
- ¼ yard (22.9cm) of heavyweight fusible interfacing
- Two 1" (2.5cm) squares of Velcro
- Optional: decorative zipper pull

TOOLS

- Universal needle
- Rotary cutter
- Sewing scissors
- Thread to match
- Bias tape maker

CUTTING LIST

- From first print:
  - 1 rectangle, 13" x 7" (33 x 17.8cm), for front pocket
  - 1 rectangle, 13" x 11¾" (33 x 29.8cm), for back
  - 1 rectangle, 3" x 2" (7.6 x 5.1cm), for zipper tab

- From second print:
  - 1 rectangle, 13" x 8½" (33 x 21.6cm), for front
  - 1 rectangle, 13" x 8½" (33 x 21.6cm), for front lining
- From third print:
  - 1 rectangle, 13" x 7" (33 x 17.8cm), for back pocket
- From fourth print:
  - 1 rectangle, 13" x 11¾" (33 x 29.8cm), for back lining
  - 1 rectangle, 13" x 7" (33 x 17.8cm), for back pocket lining
  - 1 rectangle, 13" x 7" (33 x 17.8cm), for front pocket lining
- From fifth print:
  - Multiple strips, 2" (5.1cm) wide, enough for 39" (99.1cm) of binding
- From interfacing:
  - 1 rectangle, 13" x 11¾" (33 x 29.8cm)
  - 1 rectangle, 13" x 8½" (33 x 21.6cm)
  - 2 rectangles, 13" x 7" (33 x 17.8cm)

FIG. 1

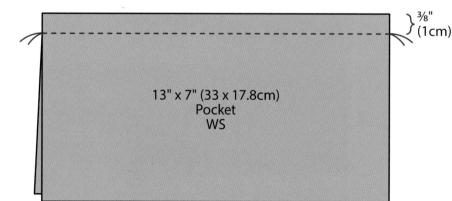

13" x 7" (33 x 17.8cm)
Pocket
WS

⅜"
(1cm)

1. Fuse 13" x 7" (33 x 17.8cm) interfacing rectangles to the pocket lining pieces.

2. With wrong sides together, stitch across the top edge with a ⅜" (1cm) seam allowance (fig. 1).

Tip

Keep important documents safely tucked away inside the zipper pocket, and items you use frequently in the front pockets.

FIG. 2

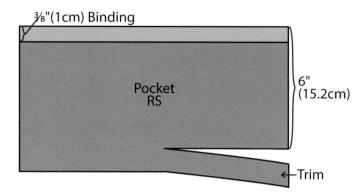

⅜"(1cm) Binding

Pocket
RS

6"
(15.2cm)

←Trim

3. Press the seam allowance toward the lining, then fold the lining to the outer fabric with wrong sides together, creating a ⅜" (1cm) binding at the top of the pocket. Press. Trim the lower edges even to create a 6" (15.2cm)–deep pocket (fig. 2). Baste across the lower edges through all layers.

FIG. 3A

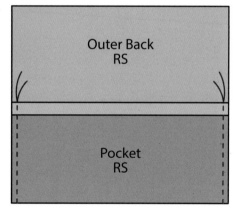

Outer Back
RS

Pocket
RS

FIG. 3B

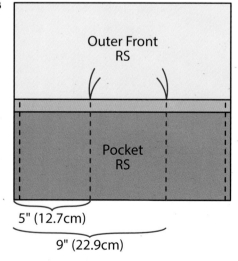

Outer Front
RS

Pocket
RS

5" (12.7cm)

9" (22.9cm)

4. Place the back pocket on the outer back rectangle piece, aligning the lower raw edges and side edges. Pin and baste on each side with a ⅜" (1cm) seam allowance (fig. 3a). Repeat with the front pocket and the outer front rectangle. Determine how wide you would like each pocket section to be. On the caddy shown, the first pocket stitch line is 5" (12.7cm) from the left side, and the second stitch line is 9" (22.9cm) from the left side, creating two miscellaneous pockets and a glasses-sized pocket (fig. 3b). Using a clear ruler and wash-away marker, draw your pocket stitch lines and topstitch directly on the lines; backstitch at the top to secure.

FIG. 4

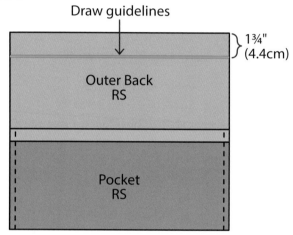

Draw guidelines

1¾"
(4.4cm)

Outer Back
RS

Pocket
RS

5. Fuse the 13" x 11¾" (33 x 29.8cm) interfacing rectangle to the back lining piece. Using a clear ruler and a wash-away marker, draw a horizontal line 1¾" (4.4cm) from the top edge of the outer back rectangle (fig. 4).

FIG. 5

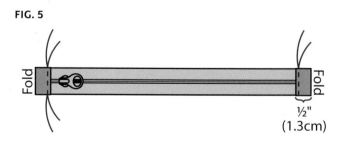

Fold

Fold

½"
(1.3cm)

6. Trim the zipper to 13" (33cm) long. Fold back ½" (1.3cm) on each short end of your zipper tab rectangle. Fold it in half so the pressed edges meet. Insert the zipper into the center of the tab; you should have approximately ½" (1.3cm) of the tab extending from each side. Stitch across the tab over the zipper with a scant ⅛" (0.3cm) seam allowance. Trim the tab flush with the zipper on each side (fig. 5).

FIG. 6

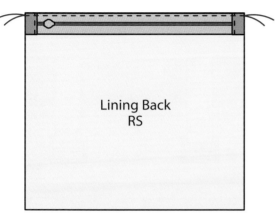

Lining Back
RS

7. Unzip the zipper about 2" (5cm). Place the zipper wrong side down on the top of the back lining rectangle as shown. Using a zipper foot on your sewing machine, baste to join the zipper to the lining using a ¼" (0.6cm) seam allowance (fig 6).

FIG. 7

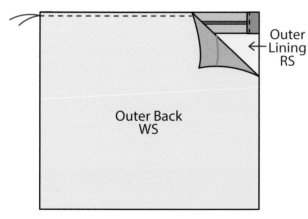

Outer Lining RS

Outer Back
WS

8. Place the outer back rectangle right sides together, aligning the top edges and sandwiching the zipper between. Pin. Stitch through all layers. Once you've stitched past the beginning of the zipper tape approximately 1" (2.5cm), raise the presser foot with the needle down. Zip the zipper closed, then continue stitching to the end. Backstitch to secure (fig. 7).

FIG. 8

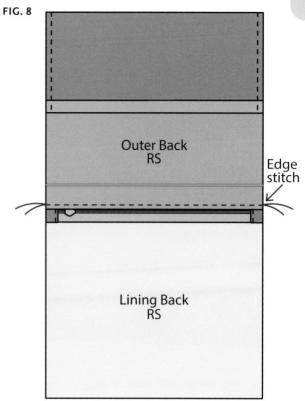

Outer Back
RS

Edge
stitch

Lining Back
RS

9. Press the outer fabric away from the zipper and press the lining fabric down. Topstitch a scant ⅛" (0.3cm) on the outer fabric next to the zipper (fig. 8).

FIG. 9

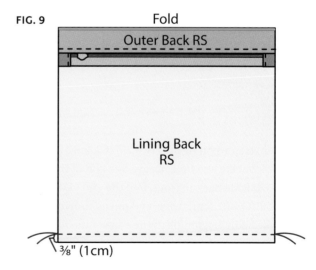

Fold

Outer Back RS

Lining Back
RS

⅜" (1cm)

10. Fold the outer back rectangle on the line traced in step 6, wrong side of outer back to wrong side of lining. Press along the folded edge. Pin and trim both fabrics even at the bottom so your joined section measures 9½" (23.5cm) long. Baste along the bottom with a ⅜" (1cm) seam allowance (fig. 9).

11. Fuse the interfacing to the front lining rectangle. Apply the front lining and outer front to the remaining side of the zipper, following the technique detailed in steps 6 through 9. True up the bottom edges of the front with the back.

FIG. 10A

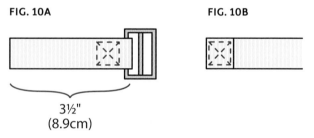

3½"
(8.9cm)

FIG. 10B

12. Cut your strap webbing into two 25" (63.5cm) pieces. Working one buckle at a time, weave one end of the strap through the buckle back to front, fold the end of the strap back on itself 1¼" (3.2cm) twice, and pin as shown in fig. 10a. Stitch a square beginning at the edge of the folded back end, finishing with an X in the center of the square (fig. 10a). Finish the remaining raw end of the strap by folding back and stitching in the same manner (fig. 10b). Repeat for the second strap and buckle. Cut the straps so that the piece with the buckle measures approximately 3½" (8.9cm) from the end of the buckle to the end of the strap, so you will have two short buckle pieces and two longer straps with one finished end.

FIG. 11

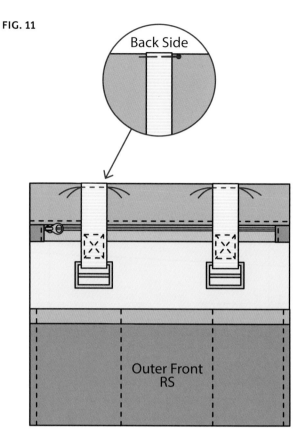

13. Position the straps with the buckles on the caddy front, facing down with the straps' raw ends even with the top edge of the caddy and 2½" (6.4cm) in from each side. Pin. Position the raw ends of the longer straps directly behind the buckle straps, again with raw edges aligned with the top of the caddy (the caddy is sandwiched between the straps). Stitch across the straps ⅜" (1cm) from the raw edges to attach (fig. 11).

FIG. 12

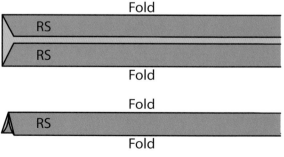

14. Join your 2" (5.1cm)–wide binding strips together; refer to Joining Binding Ends on page 22. Fold each long side of your binding strip to the wrong side ½" (1.3cm) to meet at the center. Press. Fold in half again to create ½" (1.3cm) double-fold binding. It's important to fold the sides and press evenly so your binding will be uniform (fig. 12).

FIG. 13

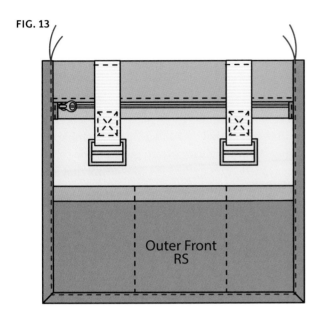

Outer Front
RS

15. Starting at the top side edge, insert the caddy raw edge into the binding, making sure the edge of the caddy is nested in the inside center fold of the binding. Glue or baste the binding to both sides of the caddy all the way around to the opposite side edge, mitering the binding at the corners (fig. 13). Make sure you have an even ½" (1.3cm) width of binding on both sides of the caddy. Trim off the excess binding and set aside for the top edge. Edge stitch the binding to attach. Before stitching all the way around, make sure you're catching both sides of your binding in the stitch line. If not, move your needle to adjust the positioning.

FIG. 14

Fold

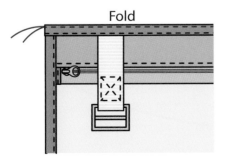

16. Measure across the top of your caddy and cut the remaining binding strip to this measurement plus ⅝" (1.6cm). Open and fold back the raw short ends ¼" (0.6cm) and press. Fold the binding over the top edge as you did for the caddy sides and apply, making sure the finished binding ends are flush with the side of the caddy (fig. 14).

FIG. 15

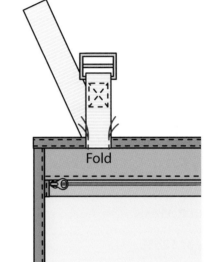

Fold

17. Fold the webbing straps up and press them flat against the binding on both sides. Pin and edge stitch along the sides of the webbing to secure (fig. 15).

FIG. 16

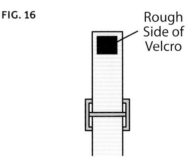

Rough Side of Velcro

18. Weave the long strap end through the buckle and adhere the rough side of the square of Velcro on the inside edge of the webbing. The Velcro will stick to the webbing and keep it in place (fig. 16).

Patterns

All of the patterns for this book are on the following pages. The patterns provided are shown at a reduced size to fit the page. Each pattern piece will need to be scaled to full size when photocopied. To ensure your pattern has printed properly, measure the 1" (2.5cm) reference block prior to use.

To skip scaling and photocopying, a PDF download of all the pattern pieces in this section is available at the link below to print on standard 8.5" x 11" paper using your home printer. (If you do not already have a PDF reader software, you can download a free one such as Adobe Reader before downloading the PDF.) Follow the guidelines at right for successful printing.

http://foxchapelpublishing.com/ Landauer/sewing-care-patterns

Here are some important notes to keep in mind when working with the patterns:

- Before beginning, read all notes and instructions not only on the patterns themselves, but also in the project text. Make sure you understand all markings and notes.

- All pattern pieces **in the downloadable patterns only** are given at 100% full size; simply print them out on 8.5" x 11" sheets of paper. Make sure that when you print, you select "actual size"; do not scale or shrink to fit the page.

- Several projects' patterns are too large to print full-size on a standard printer. These patterns have been tiled into multiple pieces that you will need to assemble before cutting out your fabric pattern pieces. Tape the paper pieces together on both sides and ensure that all edges and indicator arrows/labels are perfectly matched. Then use the pattern as normal.

Shaped Face Mask

Photocopy at 125%

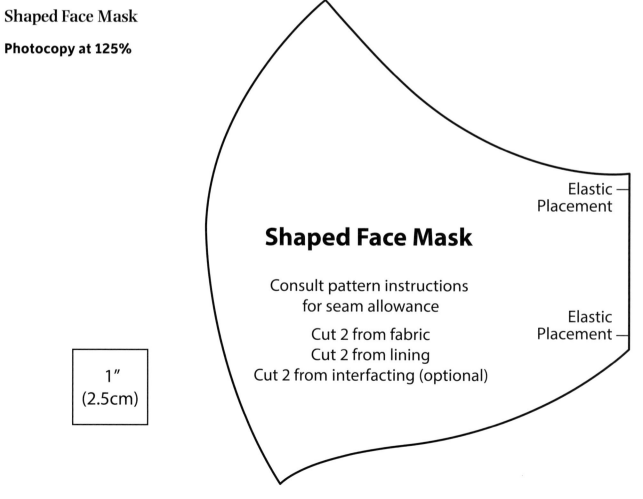

Elastic Placement

Elastic Placement

Shaped Face Mask

Consult pattern instructions
for seam allowance

Cut 2 from fabric
Cut 2 from lining
Cut 2 from interfacing (optional)

1"
(2.5cm)

Memory-Care Fidget Mat

Photocopy at 100%

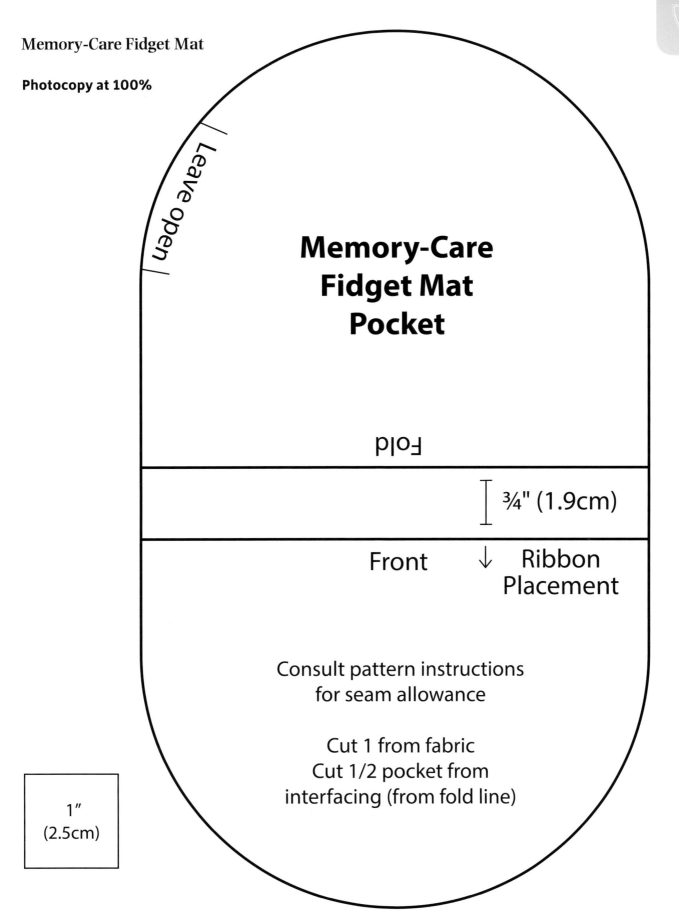

Leave open

Memory-Care Fidget Mat Pocket

Fold

¾" (1.9cm)

Front ↓ Ribbon Placement

Consult pattern instructions for seam allowance

Cut 1 from fabric
Cut 1/2 pocket from interfacing (from fold line)

1"
(2.5cm)

Ponytail Scrub Cap

Align pieces at arrows as shown and tape.

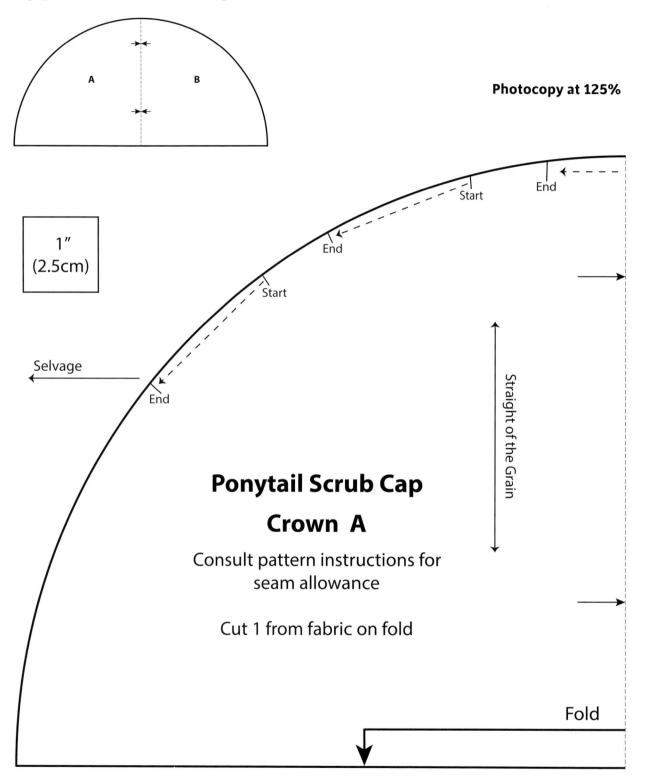

Photocopy at 125%

A   B

1″
(2.5cm)

Start

End

Start

End

Selvage

End

Straight of the Grain

Ponytail Scrub Cap

Crown A

Consult pattern instructions for
seam allowance

Cut 1 from fabric on fold

Fold

Ponytail Scrub Cap

Photocopy at 125%

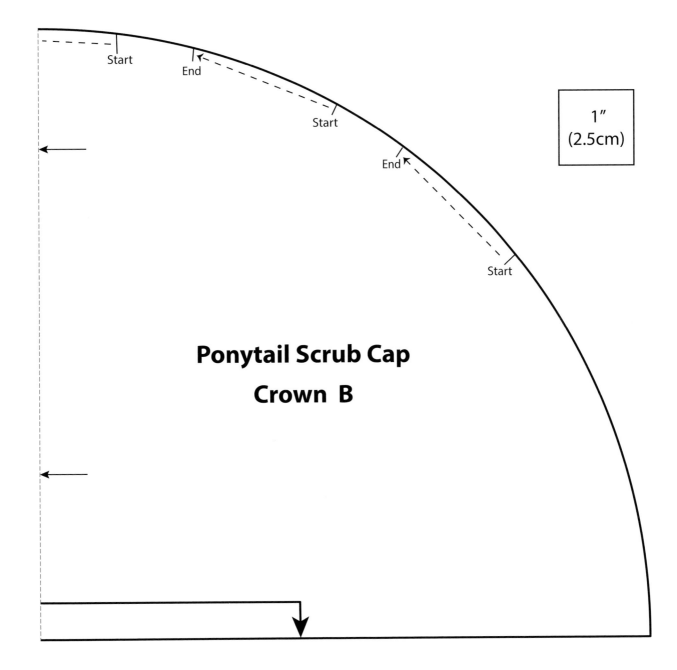

Start

End

Start

End

Start

1"
(2.5cm)

Ponytail Scrub Cap

Crown B

Fat Quarter Scrub Cap

Photocopy at 125%

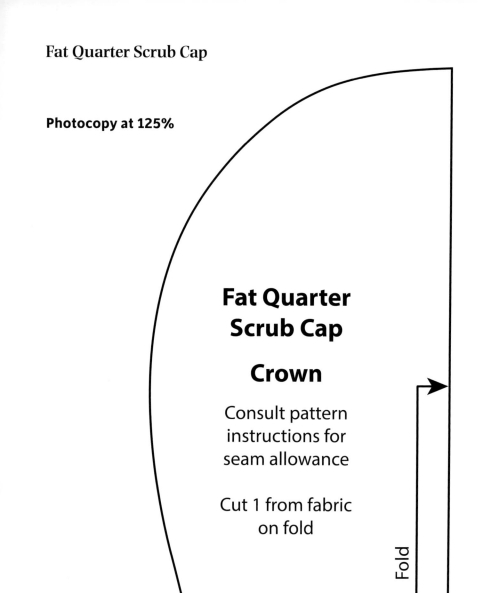

Fat Quarter Scrub Cap

Crown

Consult pattern instructions for seam allowance

Cut 1 from fabric on fold

Fold

1"
(2.5cm)

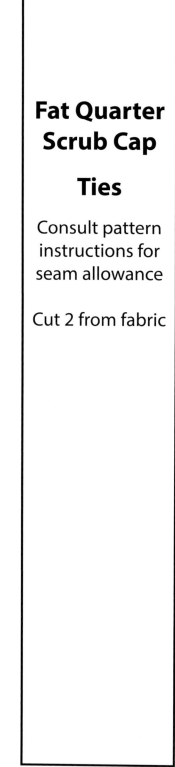

Fat Quarter Scrub Cap

Ties

Consult pattern instructions for seam allowance

Cut 2 from fabric

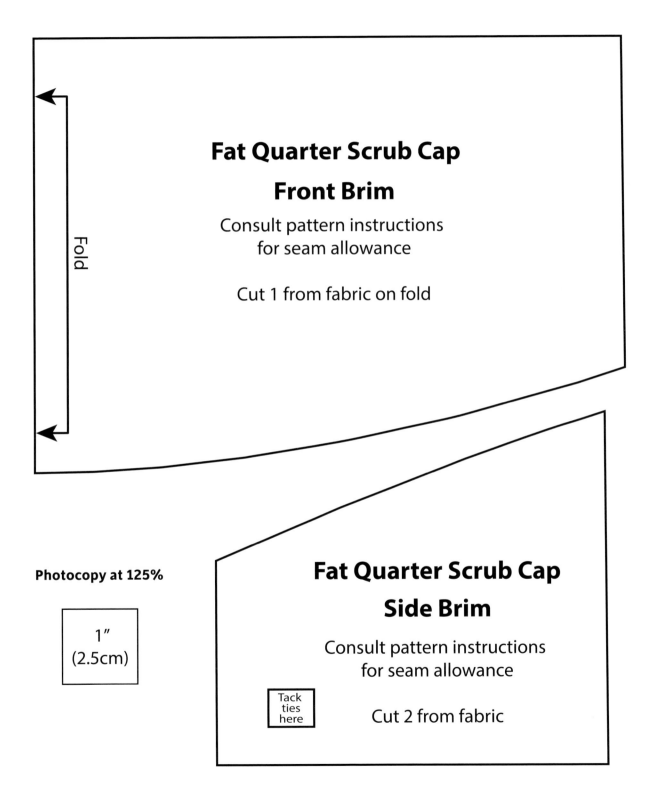

Fat Quarter Scrub Cap

Front Brim

Consult pattern instructions
for seam allowance

Cut 1 from fabric on fold

Fold

Photocopy at 125%

1"
(2.5cm)

Fat Quarter Scrub Cap

Side Brim

Consult pattern instructions
for seam allowance

Cut 2 from fabric

Tack
ties
here

Stretch Knit Face Covering/Scarf

Align pieces at arrows as shown and tape.

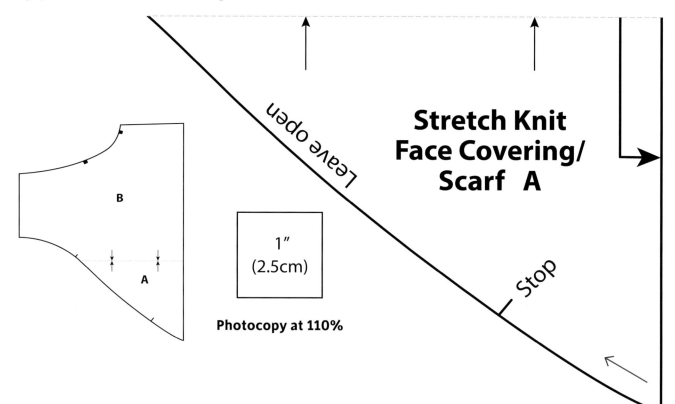

Leave open

Stretch Knit Face Covering/ Scarf A

B

A

1"
(2.5cm)

Photocopy at 110%

Stop

Arm Sling Cast Cover

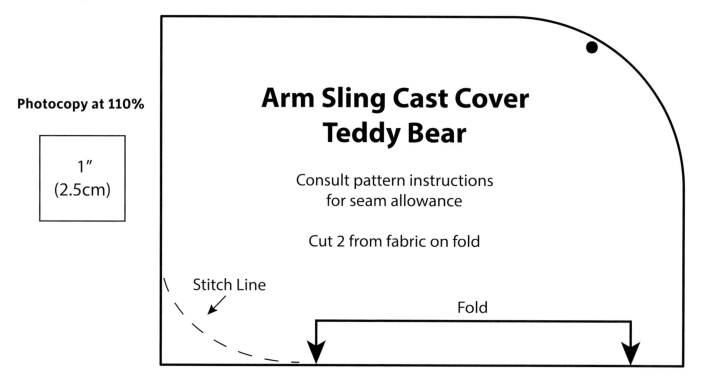

Photocopy at 110%

1"
(2.5cm)

Arm Sling Cast Cover
Teddy Bear

Consult pattern instructions
for seam allowance

Cut 2 from fabric on fold

Stitch Line

Fold

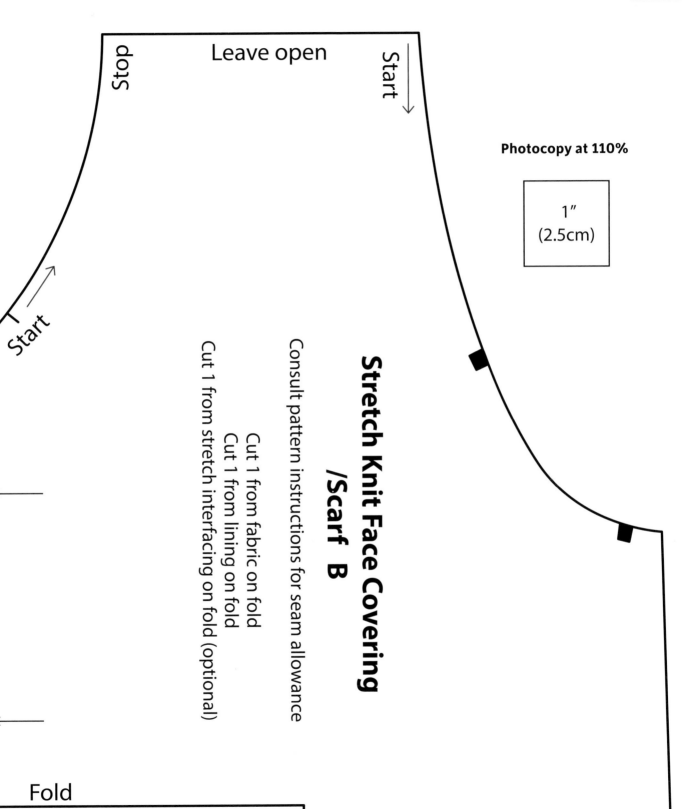

Leave open

Stop

Start

Start

Photocopy at 110%

1"
(2.5cm)

**Stretch Knit Face Covering
/Scarf B**

Consult pattern instructions for seam allowance

Cut 1 from fabric on fold
Cut 1 from lining on fold
Cut 1 from stretch interfacing on fold (optional)

Fold

Arm Sling Cast Cover

Photocopy at 100%

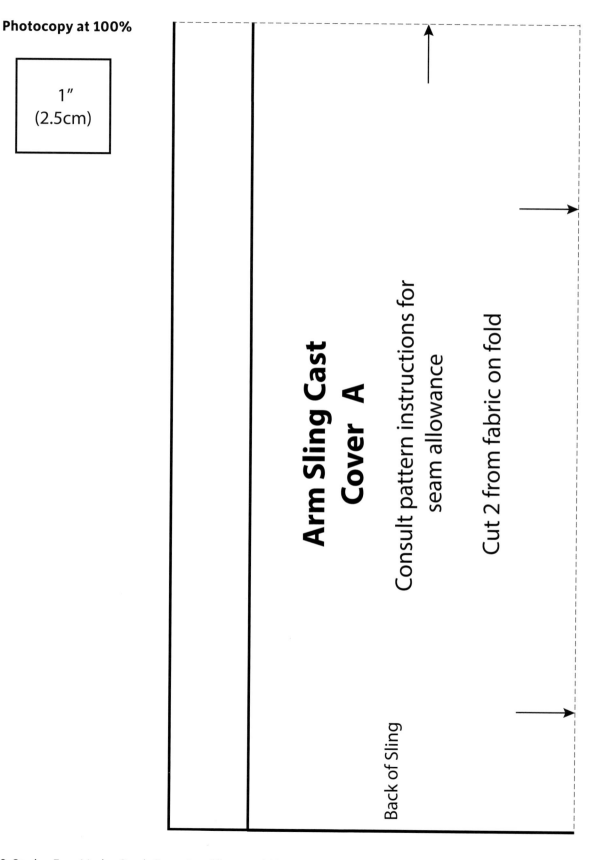

1″
(2.5cm)

Arm Sling Cast Cover A

Consult pattern instructions for seam allowance

Cut 2 from fabric on fold

Back of Sling

Arm Sling Cast Cover

Align pieces at arrows as shown and tape.

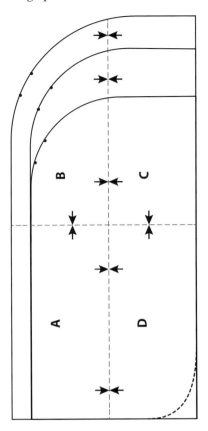

B

C

A

D

Photocopy at 100%

1"
(2.5cm)

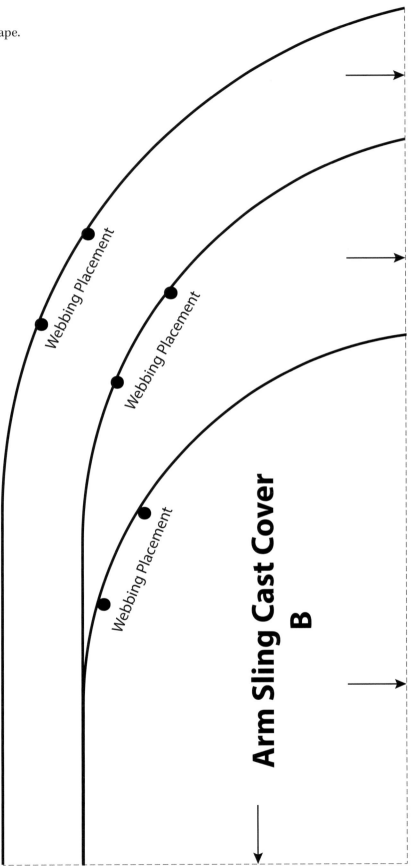

Webbing Placement

Webbing Placement

Webbing Placement

Arm Sling Cast Cover B

Arm Sling Cast Cover

Photocopy at 100%

1"
(2.5cm)

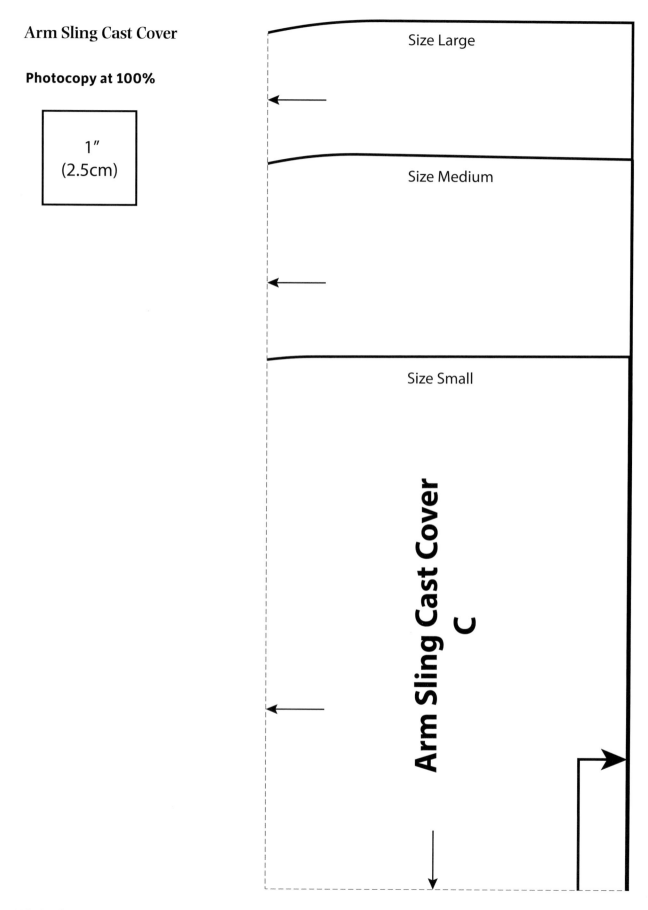

Size Large

Size Medium

Size Small

**Arm Sling Cast Cover
C**

Arm Sling Cast Cover

Photocopy at 100%

1"
(2.5cm)

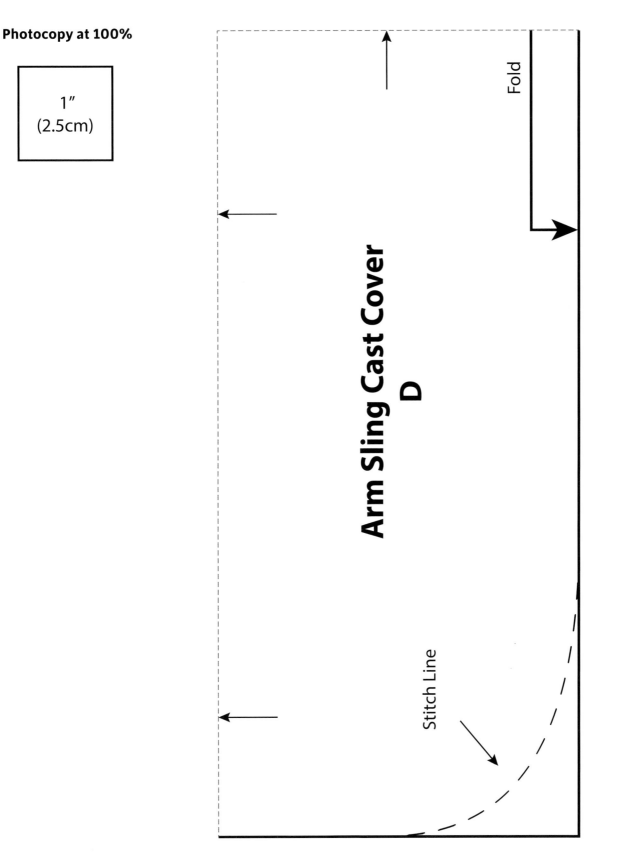

**Arm Sling Cast Cover
D**

Fold

Stitch Line

Cheery Adult Bib

Align pieces at arrows as shown and tape.

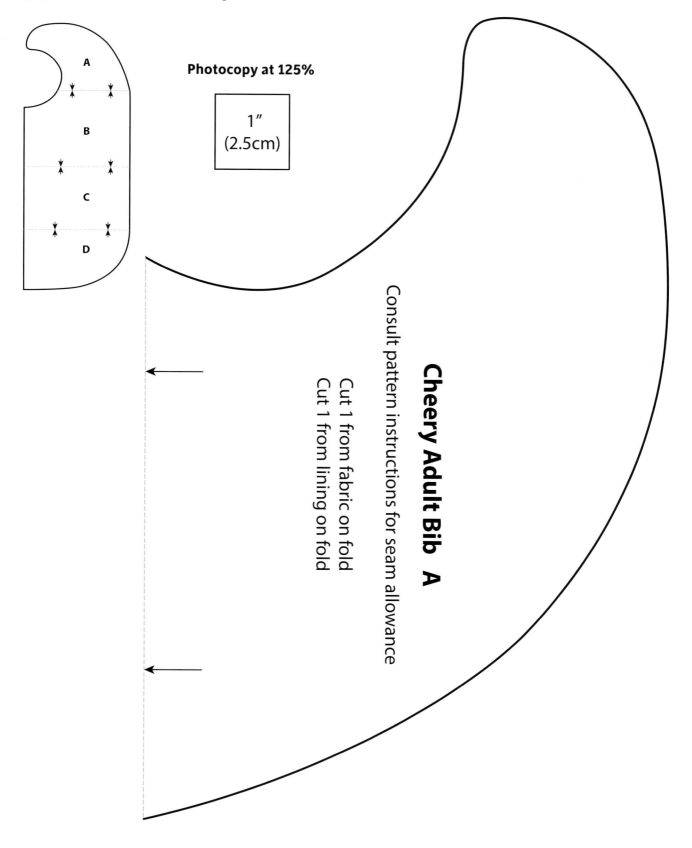

A

B

C

D

Photocopy at 125%

1"
(2.5cm)

Cheery Adult Bib A

Consult pattern instructions for seam allowance

Cut 1 from fabric on fold
Cut 1 from lining on fold

Cheery Adult Bib

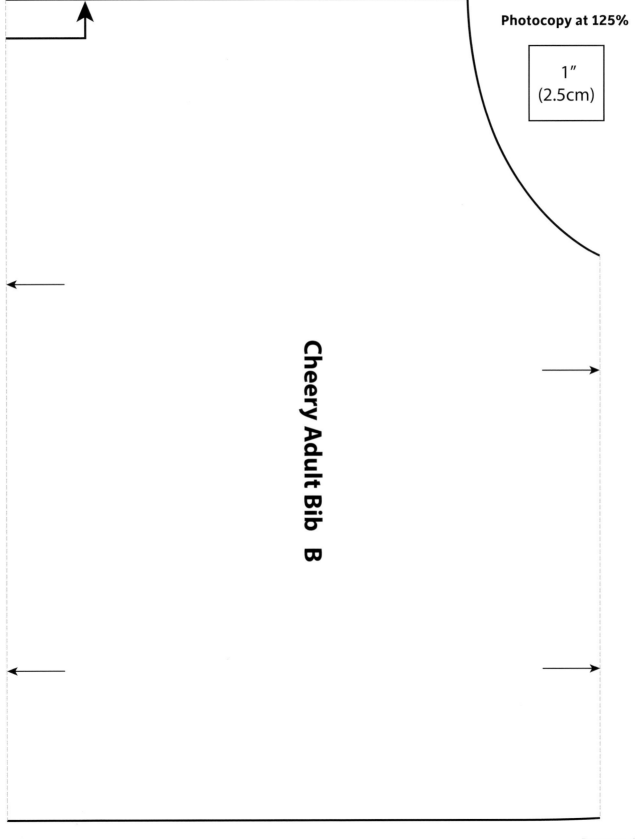

Photocopy at 125%

1″
(2.5cm)

Cheery Adult Bib B

Cheery Adult Bib

Photocopy at 125%

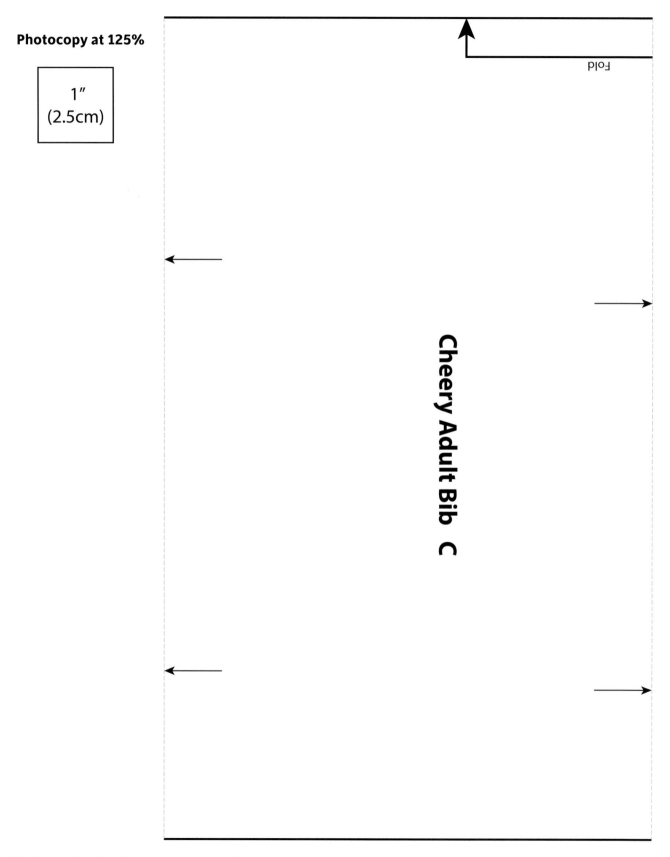

1″
(2.5cm)

Fold

Cheery Adult Bib   C

Cheery Adult Bib

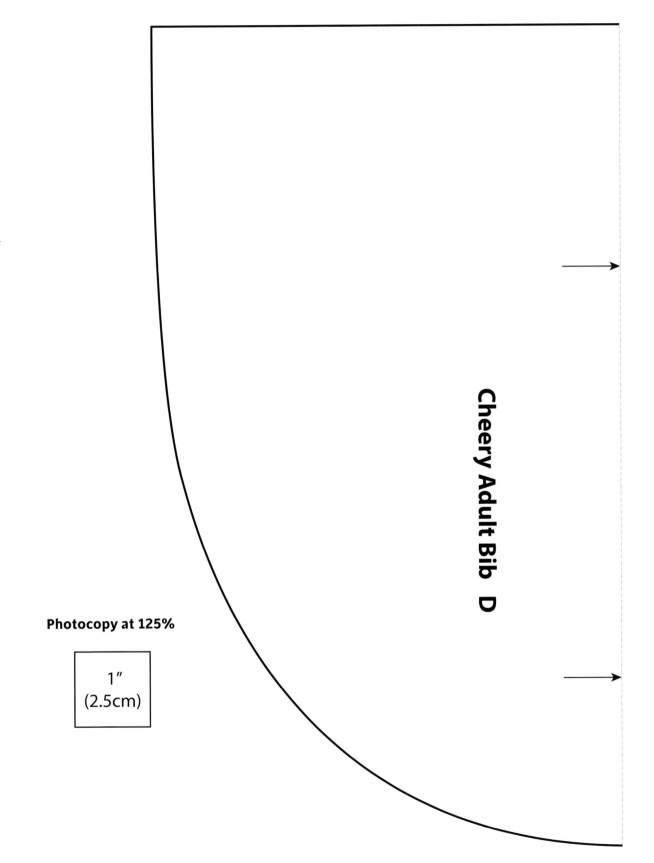

Cheery Adult Bib D

Photocopy at 125%

1"
(2.5cm)

Cooper Unisex Scrub Cap

Align pieces at arrows as shown and tape.

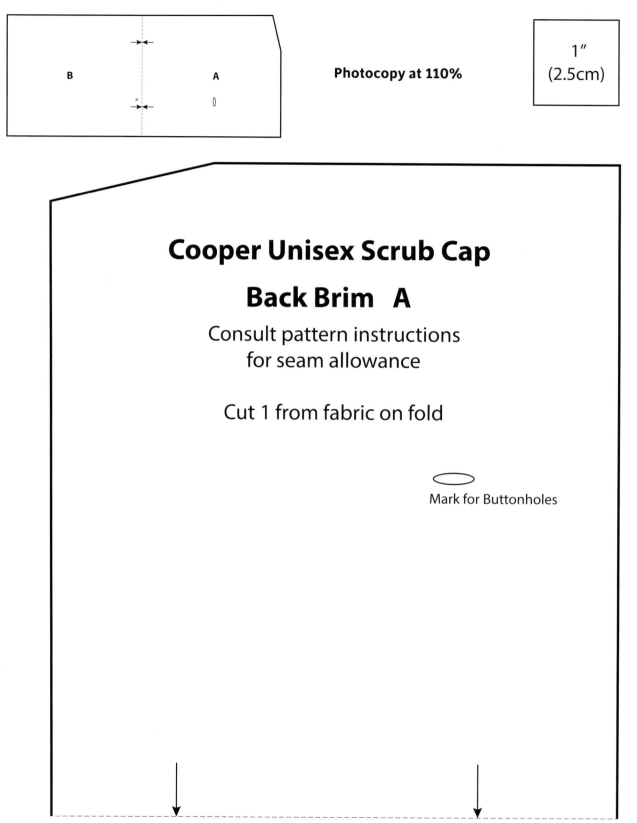

Photocopy at 110%

1"
(2.5cm)

Cooper Unisex Scrub Cap

Back Brim   A

Consult pattern instructions
for seam allowance

Cut 1 from fabric on fold

Mark for Buttonholes

Cooper Unisex Scrub Cap

Photocopy at 110%

1"
(2.5cm)

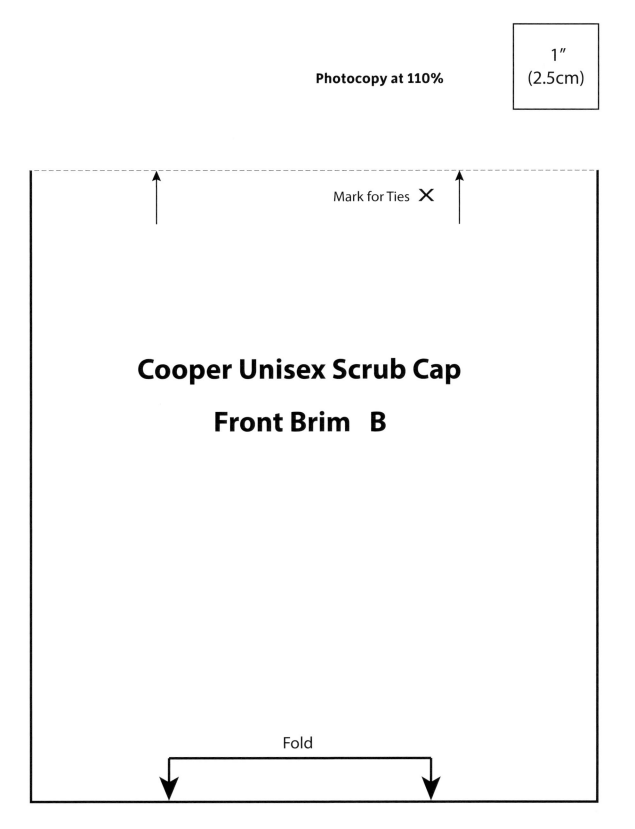

Mark for Ties ✗

Cooper Unisex Scrub Cap

Front Brim   B

Fold

Photocopy at 125%

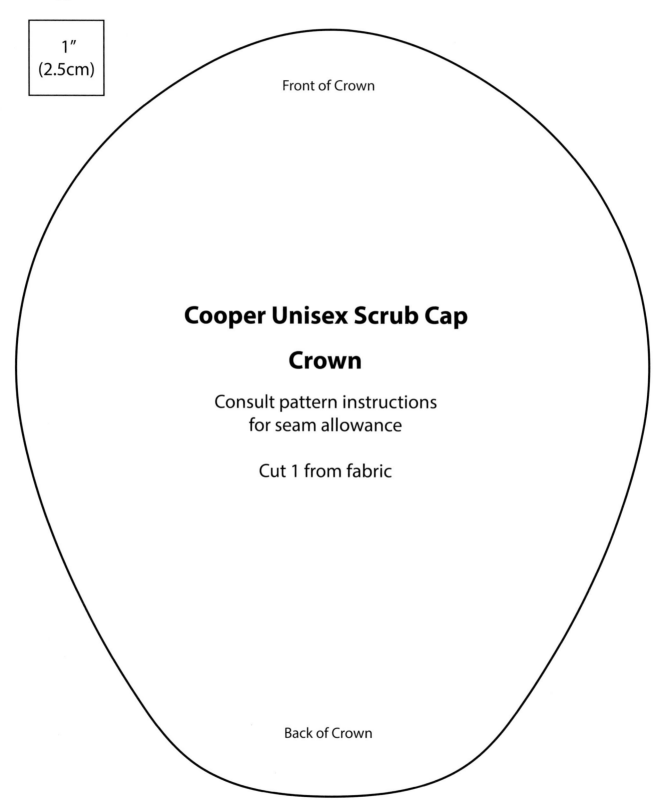

1"
(2.5cm)

Front of Crown

Cooper Unisex Scrub Cap

Crown

Consult pattern instructions
for seam allowance

Cut 1 from fabric

Back of Crown

ABOUT THE AUTHOR

Angie Herbertson has always loved creating things with her hands—from sewing, stained glass, and mosaics to crochet, graphic design, and the list goes on. She is a pattern designer, artist, and owner of an online business since 2004, A Design By Angie, where she is most notable for her inventive scrub hat patterns that come in a variety of unique yet practical styles. The idea for her online shop came about one night while she was trying to sew a scrub hat for her neighbor. She had hoped to find a sewing pattern download to make the process easier, but couldn't find one. She realized then she could simply do the work and make a scrub hat pattern herself so anyone else could have it when they needed it. Two patterns have since turned into 12 and she has more than 49,000 online sales and counting! With a passion for creating new, thoughtful things and helping others do the same, she strives to make the world a better place with color and creativity. To see her designs and easy-to-follow tutorials, visit her Etsy shop (A Design By Angie) or her website, *www.scrubhatpatterns.com.*

ACKNOWLEDGMENTS

First and foremost, I want to thank God, because His grace and mercy is new and fresh every day. I'm thankful for my husband and our children. I'm not exactly certain how he puts up with me and all my idiosyncrasies, but I'm so glad he does, and I love that handsome man. I'm thankful for Debbie and that two-day crash course she gave me in sewing all those years ago, and I only wish I could do as much as she believes I can. I want to thank Norma, my sweet nurse friend, who started me on the scrub hat pattern journey, way back then. My sister Beth, my friend Angela, and my mom are always so excited and supportive of every new thing I do. My sweet cousin Keith always pops up in just the right places in life, and his sweetness just makes my heart full. Nancy...for just being you, always being the voice of reason, and taking a chance on me. I could seriously go on and on, because I've been blessed so many ways by a loving family, fabulous friends who love deeply, and a wonderfully supportive and amazing church family.

Last, but not least, I want to thank my editor, Amelia. She was just browsing the Internet one day and decided to take a chance on me. She probably doesn't realize just how much that meant to me.

Photo Credits

The following images are credited to their respective creators: materials and tools photos on pp. 10–16: Amelia Johanson; step-by-step illustrations: Sue Friend; project photos: Mike Mihalo; author photo on p. 119: Carli Herbertson

The following images are credited to Shutterstock.com and their respective creators: front cover: AVAVA; p. 4: triocean; p. 5: Monkey Business Images; p. 8: Szasz-Fabian Ilka Erika; pp. 8–9: Ekramar; p. 17: White bear studio; p. 24 (button): triocean; p. 24 (scissors): Oleksandr Kostiuchenko; pp. 24–25: JasminkaM; p. 65 (bed background): Arkhipenko Olga; burlap background on p. 26 and throughout: Vladimir Prusakov; icons on p. 1 and throughout: Milta

INDEX

Note: Page numbers in *italics* indicate projects and (patterns).